HOURS

OF

SPIRITUAL REFRESHMENT

BY

DR. HENRY MUELLER

TRANSLATED FROM THE GERMAN

BY THE

REV. MAXIMILIAN GENESTE, M. A.,

Original Publishing Info:

LONDON:
THE RELIGIOUS TRACT SOCIETY;
Instituted 1799
THE DEPOSITORY, 56, PATERNOSTER ROW, AND 65, ST. PAUL'S
CHURCHYARD

www.JustandSinner.com

HOURS OF SPIRITUAL REFRESHMENR
By Henry Mueller

Just & Sinner
425 East Lincoln Ave.
Watseka, IL 60970

www.JustandSinner.com

ISBN 10: 0692601694
ISBN 13: 978-0692601693

CONTENTS

PREFACE

OF all the writings of Dr. Henry Müller, which are very numerous, his "Hours of Spiritual Refreshment" have been the most highly esteemed, and frequently reprinted. Somewhat resembling, in spirit and form, the book of Ecclesiasticus, or even the Proverbs of Solomon, they contain a treasure, both of inward and outward experience, and of Christian wisdom; the style and manner being perfectly original—at once brief, pointed, and energetic, as well as lively, diversified, and serious.

This high estimation of the work has been expressed by many. The writer of a preface to an edition published in 1686, exclaims, in a tone of joyful surprise, "Yes, precious little book, what I have heard in my own country respecting thy worth and wisdom is true; yet I could not believe till I had seen it with mine eyes; and behold! not the half had been told me. Thy fame, great as it is, does not equal thy merit. Happy are the men who stand before thee, and hear thy wisdom."

Similar testimony may be adduced of the value attached to this work in the present day, but one reference may suffice: "I know of no modern publication of the same kind," says a learned divine in Hamburgh, "which I can compare with Müller's, for brevity, depth, and power."

The present selection from the "Hours of Spiritual Refreshment," it is hoped, will answer its original intention, in the correction, reproof, edification, and comfort of many. It certainly will profit all its readers, of whatever class and condition of men, whose hearts are under the teaching of the Spirit of God.

A BRIEF MEMOIR

OF

DR. HENRY MÜLLER

HENRY MÜLLER was born in the Hanseatic town of Lübeck, on the 18th of October, 1631. To this place his parents had fled for refuge, when, after the defeat of the King of Denmark, the flood of war rolled over the territory of Mecklenburg; and it was here, whilst the desolating contest ravaged the whole of Germany, from the Danube to the shores of the Baltic, indicating the chastening hand of God, that he was trained up, by his pious parents, in the nurture and admonition of the Lord.

His father, Peter Müller, a merchant and citizen of Rostock, was a man of irreproachable life and conversation; his mother, Elizabeth, was eminent for her virtues, and applied herself with the diligence which distinguished the mothers of St. Chrysostom and St. Augustine, to imbue the mind of her child with the principles of true religion, and fill his soul with the love of Christ. The boy, though of a weakly frame, gave early tokens of a lively and generous disposition, and made such attainments in wisdom and knowledge, that, like Muret, about a hundred years before, he, at an early age, seemed suited rather to be an instructor, than himself to be taught.

Having acquired the rudiments of education at Lübeck, on the return of his parents to their native place, he entered the high school, in his thirteenth year, and consecrated the first fruits of his life to the service and glory of God, as he states in a sermon, which he delivered under a deep sense of the grace which had been bestowed upon him. Instructed in classical literature by the learned rector of the high school of Rostock; guided in his philosophical studies by Lütkemann, a deep thinker and Christian theologian, who used to say, "I had rather be the means of saving one soul, than making a hundred learned," and having made great proficiency in the oriental languages, under the celebrated Fabricius of Westphalia, he repaired, by the advice of the venerable Quirtorp, to the university of Greifswalde, where he further prosecuted his studies for three years, and engaged in four public disputations, in which he acquitted himself so as to attract considerable attention. On his return to Rostock, he held two public disputations under the presidency of Varenius, and had the degree of master of arts conferred upon him in his seventeenth year, as an honorable token of his distinguished learning and ability.

This period of his life was devoted to the strenuous pursuit of knowledge; for, in order to perfect himself in his theological studies, and secure the friendship of those who were eminent alike as scholars and divines, he visited in succession the universities of Dantzic, Königsberg, Helmstädt, Leipzig, and Wittenberg. The names of Botsack, Mislente, George Calixtus, Carpzovius, Calovius, and Meisner, attracted him to these seats of learning. To Leipzig he was particularly attached; he there lived with Carpzovius, and was on terms of friendly intercourse with Lange, Hülsemann, and Geier. From thence, at the request of his parents, he removed to Rostock, where he delivered a course of profound and original lectures to the students, composed and published two beautiful treatises, (Methodus Politica, and Orator Ecclesiasticus,) and laid the foundation of that high estimation, in which he was deservedly held for spiritual attainments, and pulpit eloquence.

As a Christian orator, Müller was distinguished for judgment, knowledge of the Scriptures, power of thought, and brevity of expression. The senate of the city, fully convinced of his piety and theological attainments, conferred on him the archdeaconry, with the church of St. Mary, in Rostock, in his 20th year; and he soon after married Margaret Elizabeth, the only daughter of Siebrands, a citizen and merchant of the same place. Their union, which continued for twenty-two years of uninterrupted happiness, was blessed with five sons and one daughter: whilst the duties of his high office were discharged with diligence and fidelity; and the strong, pointed, and spiritual enforcement of Divine truth, by which he sought to lead his people in the way of life, was enforced by his own example. "I well remember," he writes, "that when I entered upon that important office which I yet fill, I trembled at the responsibility, oppressed by the sense of my inexperience and insufficiency. And what did I do? I fell on my knees before God in my chamber, and said with Jeremiah, 'Ah, Lord God! behold, I cannot speak: for I am a child. But the Lord said unto me, Say not, I am a child: for thou shalt go to all that I shall send thee, and whatsoever I command thee thou shalt speak. Be not afraid of their faces: for I am with thee to deliver thee, saith the Lord.'"

Next to his ministerial duties, he prosecuted with alacrity his academic labours, and gave daily proof of the powers of his elevated mind, and of his profound erudition. The students heard him with pleasure; and many of them, under his instructions, became distinguished orators and theologians, among whom may be mentioned the celebrated Lassenius, who is said to have been "an assiduous pupil of Müller."

In 1655 he was appointed by the senate, professor extraordinary of theology, which office, however, he shortly resigned, as the arrangement did not meet with the concurrence of the duke of Mecklenburg, the patron of the university. In return, they conferred upon him, in 1659, the professorship of Greek, the degree of doctor in divinity having already been granted him by the university of Helmstädt, in the twenty-second year of his age. Subsequently, in 1662, he was appointed professor of divinity in Rostock. He was thrice rector of the academy, and filled the office of senior of the theological faculty; and lastly, by the unanimous voice, both civil and ecclesiastical, he was elected superintendent, confirmed in that high function by the duke of Mecklenburg, and solemnly installed by Sommerfeld, in Parchion, in 1671. On that important occasion he was observed to shed tears, which called forth the exclamation from Sommerfeld, "What do I see! tears in the midst of honor! I will mark it well."

His heart was in his work, and it was his unwearied endeavour, for the space of twenty-two years, not only faithfully to discharge to the glory of God his important academic and ecclesiastical duties in his native town of Rostock, but also to benefit others by his valuable publications. Several hymns, which are to be found in many collections, he published in his "Melody of the Soul," and his "School of the Cross." These show Müller to be, if not an original poet, at least a happy imitator of the best poets of the day, P. Gerhard, J. Franke, and Scheffler, in whose warm Christian feelings he largely participated; and his hymns were admired as well for their beauty and skill in composition, as for the spirit of piety which they uniformly breathe. By his ascetic and theological writings, which are marked by their scriptural tone, conciseness, and energy of expression, by their happy turn of thought, and just observation, the German language became more generally read, especially in Italy. Some of his works were translated into other languages.

Thus the name of Henry Müller attained extensive celebrity. He received many tokens of honor, and was invited to several places as superintendent or professor of divinity; whilst consistories, states, and royal personages sought his counsel and advice in cases of difficulty. An application of this description was made to him from Malaga in his last sickness; but he could never be induced to leave his native land; and though as a servant of God he was subjected to calumny and persecution, yet he stood in Mecklenburg as a towering cedar, with roots deeply bedded in the soil, unmoved by the storm which swept over him, and both friends and enemies could not but accord him the testimony of an uniformly exemplary, stedfast, and consistent Christian course.

His love to his country, and especially to his congregation and pastoral charge at Rostock, he thus characteristically describes on the occasion of an offer of preferment in Hamburgh: "I have in my native town an affectionate people, who regard me as an angel of God, who faithfully receive the word of the Lord, preached by me to their edification, and overwhelm me with benefits. What could prevail on me to forsake them I never yet have been able to imagine. Riches I have never sought: having food and raiment, I have learned therewith to be content. God be thanked, I am in want of nothing. I desire not to leave treasures to my children: what I wish for them is a believing heart, and to commit them to the care of a gracious God, amidst his loving and sympathizing people. For sloth and idleness I have always had an aversion. I know that the servant of the Lord must not slumber or sleep, but watch and labour; and I have found that I always became stronger by work. Nor do I seek a more extensive sphere: with the few thousands among whom I am placed I find enough to do, and the care of souls is a solemn charge. 'Who is sufficient for these things?' "

Like Spener, Arnd, and Franke, he enforced, both in his preaching and writings, practical and experimental Christianity. Deeply sensible of the sinful and frail state of our fallen nature, he strenuously exhorted, on Christian principles, to a life of holiness, which he exemplified in his own practice.

He wielded the sword of the Spirit with zeal and ability, like a second Luther, against all false and hypocritical professors, who had "the form of godliness, but denied the power thereof;" he contended with heretics, and especially with two notorious heresiarchs, putting them to silence, and counteracting the fatal tendency of their poisonous dogmas. And when himself accused, by one of his own name, of advancing erroneous opinions, he appealed to the judgment of the most eminent theologians, who gave the following as their unanimous decision:—

"Dr. Henry Müller has taught nothing but what is contained in the Holy Scriptures, and he who charges such teaching with error is unworthy of regard."

The names attached to this document are these:

"Cellarius, Dr. and professor at Helmstädt.
Battus, Dr. and professor at Greifswalde.
Schuckmann, Dr. and chief chaplain in ordinary at Güstrow.
Varenius, Dr. and professor at Rostock.
Hannekenius, Dr. and superintendent at Lübeck.
Gossmann, Dr. and superintendent at Stralsund."

Thus Müller sustained not the least injury from the false accusations and calumnies of men, whilst, with the zeal and faithfullness of an apostle, he exposed and attacked sin without any respect of persons. On the other hand, he knew how wisely, and tenderly, to minister to weak and feeble believers, that they might not be discouraged, but helped onward in the way. Day and night he prayed for his flock, that the Lord would turn away from them his wrathful displeasure: he besought with tears that God would bless them with spiritual mercies, and, "give the increase," since he himself, as a helpless worm, could effect nothing. "I have often overheard him," says Barclai, "with such moving and thrilling energy praying in his study, that I have been constrained, at the same time, to bow my knees to the God and Father of our Lord Jesus Christ, and to mingle my supplications with his."

Müller was a good shepherd, who cared for all the sheep over which the Holy Ghost had made him overseer, to "feed the church of God, which he hath purchased with his own blood." He continually exercised himself in the work of faith, and labour of love. He was kind and compassionate; he was just and reasonable in his feelings towards every man; full of Christian charity and benevolence, especially towards the poor; a father of the fatherless, and defender of widows. He was mighty in prayer, and powerful in intercession; ever a sympathizing comforter, and a faithful and spiritual preacher, having "an unction from the Holy One." He was indefatigable in teaching, and in his manifold labours. His care was great for the good of the souls committed to his charge; little, in comparison, for the health of his own enfeebled body.

Henry Müller died in the forty-fourth year of his age, in Christian patience and joyfullness, resting on Christ, with a hope full of immortality. Shortly before his dissolution, he gratefully partook of the supper of the Lord. Though very weak, he sang with animation several beautiful hymns. Among the rest,—

"Herr Jesu Christ, wahrer Mensch und Gott," etc.

and

"O Lamm Gottes unschuldig," etc.

He then addressed those who were collected around his bed. "Dear children, pray, pray that the will of God may be fulfilled in me; what my God wills he always done. His will—His is the best." He took leave of his beloved wife, his children, and the archdeacon Barclai, with many tears; blessing them like the dying patriarch, and exhorting them to steadfastness in the faith and fear of God. "It is not I," he said, "but my misery and sorrow, that will die. I know not that in the whole course of my life, I have had one single day of unclouded joy. Joy is reserved for that world to which I am hastening. There, unencumbered by the body of this death, I shall bow before the throne of God and of the Lamb. Be not distressed, for I know I shall soon, without a struggle, and without a care, depart to be with Christ." And so it was; for on the very same day, the 23rd of September, 1675, after praying and conversing with his family with much cheerfullness and strength on the word of God, he gently fell asleep in Jesus at five o'clock in the afternoon. The day of his death was one of universal mourning, "that such a pillar of the church had so soon fallen, that one so justly esteemed, so highly honored in the ministry, in the consistory, and in the academy, had been so early removed," though they felt assured, that to him to live having been Christ, to die was gain.

HOURS

OF

SPIRITUAL REFRESHMENT

ON CHRISTIAN JOY

"ALWAYS REJOICING," 2 Cor. 6:10. This is my motto. Why is it not yours? You mourn and repine; it is far otherwise with me. When the wicked one attempts to harass me, I boldly face him, and say, "Get thee hence, Satan. Always rejoicing, is my motto." When visited with sickness, I yield not to distress. Lazarus, whom Jesus loved, was sick, John 11:3. Love kisses the rod. Severe discipline is frequently the most beneficial. God beats with a rod, and delivers our soul from hell, Prov. 23:14. Having been so many years in good health, why should I not be content, for the honor of God, to be a few weeks sick? "What? shall we receive good at the hand of God, and shall we not receive evil?" Job 2:10. The sickness, I thank my God, extendeth not to my soul, which Jesus hath healed: and towards my body God exerciseth the most tender, providential care; as sick children possess the warmest sympathies of their parent. God strengtheneth me upon the bed of languishing; he maketh all my bed in my sickness, Psa. 41:3. What more do I need?

Should I be calumniated, I will bear it patiently. Was not Jesus himself accused of being a winebibber, a friend of publicans and sinners? Matt. 11:19. "I will cry unto God most high; unto God that performeth all things for me. He shall send from heaven, and save me from the reproach of him that would swallow me up," Psa. 57:2, 3. My conscience condemns me not, and that is better than a thousand witnesses. Should I be troubled that they speak evil of me without a cause? Oh no! I have more reason to rejoice. "Oh that mine adversary had written a book! surely I would take it upon my shoulder, and bind it as a crown to me," Job 31:35, 36. I know well what my Savior saith, "Blessed are ye, when men shall revile you, and persecute you, and shall say all manner of evil against you falsely, for my sake. Rejoice, and be exceeding glad: for great is your reward in heaven: for so persecuted they the prophets which were before you," Matt. 5:11, 12.

Do necessity and tribulation befall me? I do not despair. The member cannot fare better than the body. When all who sailed in the ship suffer loss, why should I alone escape? Let those lament who are destitute of faith. "Behold, he that keepeth Israel shall neither slumber nor sleep," Psa. 121:4. There is a God in heaven who graciously careth for me. If I have procured such sufferings by my sins, I will repent and seek for mercy through the blood of the cross. That God who hath promised grace and pardon to all penitent sinners, will not withhold them from me.

Do I lose my friend, my child, or my wife, yet will I not cast away my confidence. "The Lord gave, and the Lord hath taken away; blessed be the name of the Lord," Job 1:21. My God still remains with me. Death is only a separation, not a loss. The friend in Christ whom I loved was loved also by the Savior, and more closely allied to Him than to me. I would not withhold my friend from Jesus, nor heaven from my friend.

Am I deprived of all my possessions, I nevertheless rejoice; my goods are not my God. What do I say? *my* goods! had they been truly such, I should not have lost them. They were not mine, but God's. Why should I repine in giving back that which has been only lent to me? Yet I do not really suffer loss; I thank God for that which I possess, and have already ceased to sorrow for what I once had. "Having food and raiment I am therewith content," 1 Tim. 6:8. He who is satisfied is rich enough. A great burden is taken from me, that I may the more easily ascend to heaven. Praised be the God of my salvation. Many corn-fields are unproductive because they were too thickly sown; many beautiful boughs are broken through the weight of the fruit. I call to mind the words of my Savior, "How hardly shall they that have riches enter into the kingdom of God," Mark 10:23. The impediments being removed, the passage is more easily effected through the eye of the needle, Mark 10:25. My goods are taken from me, my care hath ceased; contempt has had its course, and yet there is no diminution of my joy. I will tell you, in a few words, what I mean; my heart is, through grace, so closely united to my God and Savior, that nothing gives me pain, but that which may be displeasing to Him.

ON

UNION WITH CHRIST

I AM black by nature, but have been renewed by grace, Sol. Song 1:5, John 15:3. Original transgression defiled me, but the blood of Jesus hath made me whiter than snow. His righteousness is my righteousness. I have washed my robes, and made them white in the blood of the Lamb, and I shall yet see him, and walk with him in white. O blessed Jesus! thou art mine, and I am thine; who can separate us? Thou art my Shepherd, I am thy sheep, and with thee find pasture. Thou art my Bridegroom, I am thy bride. Whatsoever thou art, that art thou to me, all thine is mine. Thy blessing is my blessing. Thy life is my life. Thy salvation is my salvation. Am I poor, thou art my riches; am I oppressed, thou art my succour; am I cast out, thou art my refuge; am I sorrowful, thou art my comfort and my joy.

Whatsoever I am, that am I to thee. Sin, what seekest thou in me? I belong to Jesus; in his wounds have I found salvation. Satan, get thee hence, Jesus is my shield; thy fiery darts are directed not to *me*, but *him*. O world, attempt not my destruction, if thou assault me, thou wilt dash thy head against a wall of adamant; and whom then wilt thou put to shame, me, or thyself? Death, thou art to me a messenger of mercy. Christ is my life, to die is gain; I abide in him, and he in me, and I shall possess his love for ever.

ON

FAITH AND LOVE

THE angels of God ascended and descended upon the ladder which Jacob beheld in his dream; this is a beautiful similitude of Christ. Himself God and man, he has become Mediator between both, and has formed a communication between heaven and earth; he descended at his incarnation, and ascended when he was received up in sight of his sorrowing disciples from the hill of Bethany.

The vision of Jacob furnishes also a lively representation of the Christian. For what else is our religion than our continual communication with God and our neighbor—with God through faith, with our neighbor through love?

Arise, my soul, embrace the precious Savior in the arms of faith, and say, Thou art mine, and all thine is mine; oh, how rich art thou in possessing such a Savior! Can you say, Jesus is mine, and in him all things are mine? Let the world draw near, and exhibit all its treasures; what are they but a clod of earth? That which you can show, on the other hand, is of more value than ten thousand worlds: all things with Jesus, Jesus above all things; himself all and in all. What the world presents is imperfect, what Jesus gives is perfect. The one causes thirst, the other quenches it; the one occasions disquietude, the other conveys to us the blessings of peace. Jesus is mine, and in him all things are mine. He is my light in darkness, that I may not err; my righteousness from sin, my blessing from the curse, my life from death, my salvation from destruction, my refuge in distress, my joy in sorrow, my fullness in want, my only one, for out of him I desire nothing; my all, for in him I find all things. "The Lord is my shepherd, I shall not want."

Go forth, my soul, and embrace the lowly Jesus in the arms of love. Behold him hungry and thirsty, in sorrow, in nakedness, and misery, before your eyes. Can you suffer *him* to hunger, who supplies your daily bread, and feeds your soul with the hidden manna? Can you allow *him* to thirst, who giveth you to drink out of the rivers of his pleasure? Can you leave *him* to sorrow and to weep, who so abundantly comforts you, and wipes away all tears from your eyes? Can you permit *him* to go naked, who covers you with the garment of salvation, and with the robe of his righteousness? And can you allow *him* to be in destitution and wretchedness, who took upon him your miserable condition, that you might enter into his joy? Oh no! I will go to him, and say, "All that I have is thine; if thou art hungry, I will feed thee; if thirsty, I will give thee drink; if naked, I will clothe thee; if in distress, I will comfort thee." And he is content with a little. A crust of bread satisfies his hunger, a cup of cold water his thirst, and he desires no more than homely clothing; but if you have nothing, speak to him at least a word of comfort. To him you owe all things, from him you have received them all, and yet he will reward you by his grace, and say, "Inasmuch as ye have done it unto one of the least of these my brethren, ye have done it unto me," Matt. 25:40.

I will, in a few words, explain to you what I mean. In Christ, that faith alone which worketh by love is of any avail. Faith makes, love manifests, the Christian. The former draws us to God, the latter to our neighbor; the former receives, the latter dispenses; what faith experiences, God communicates; love conveys the blessing conferred, that it may be shared by our neighbor. The more abundantly you are enriched, the more largely you should bestow. If you would be a Christian, dispense outwardly to men that which you receive inwardly from God.

Be as a tree whose roots are in heaven, and which beareth fruit on earth. God will water it, and give the increase. Then shall your neighbor pluck thereof, and eat.

ON THE

STATE OF THE CHRISTIAN UPON EARTH

"As a rose among the thorns;"—thus do I behold the Christian upon earth. He is a fragrant rose, but among thorns; he is assaulted and beset by the devil and his angels. The world cannot endure the Savior. The Jews crucified him in his person; the world still crucifies him in his members. Doth Christ, the blessed Seed of the woman, dwell in you? Then is the accursed seed of the serpent against you, and endeavors to infliction deadly wound after another. You seek happiness in Christ—it is well. But if you call that happiness which is pleasing to the flesh, you deceive yourself, and act as foolishly as if you were to look for grapes on thorns, or figs on thistles. Christ comes not to bestow upon the flesh rich domains and luxurious living, but he enjoins mortification, and requires us to bear the cross. "They that are Christ's have crucified the flesh with the affections and lusts," Gal. 5:24. Are you a disciple of Jesus, then must you take up your cross, and follow him. "Where I am," saith he, "there shall also my servant be," John 12:26. This refers as well to a state of humiliation, as a state of glory. For we must first suffer with him, if we would be glorified together. Where do you find Jesus in his humiliation? Not in riches, but in want: He who possesseth all things had not where to lay his head: not in great honor, but in ignominy and contempt; he was "a reproach of men, and despised of the people" Psa. 22:6; not in joy and gladness, but in sorrow and in tears. "The servant is not greater than his Lord, nor the disciple than his Master," Matt. 10:24. It would be a shame to behold the servant mounted, and his Master on foot; to see the disciple encircled with a chaplet of roses, when his Master was crowned with thorns. You are not better than your Savior. Why then do you seek a better state on earth? When Uriah was bid to go to his house, he replied, "The ark, and Israel, and Judah, abide in tents; and my lord Joab, and the servants of my lord, are encamped in the open fields; shall I then go into mine house, to eat and to drink, and to lie with my wife? as thou livest, and as thy soul liveth, I will not do this thing," 2 Sam. 11:11. If the world invites you to come and enjoy its pleasures, saying, that with Christ is only sorrow; let this be your answer, "My Savior has been sorrowful, even unto death, and should I indulge in vain amusements? my Savior has wept, and should I thus laugh? No, that be far from me." If you would be a Christian, prepare yourself for the cross. The church is the body, Christ is the Head. How can the body be well if the Head suffer? Are you a member of the body of Christ, then must you also participate in the sufferings of Jesus, otherwise you are not a living but a dead member. I will not be reluctant to suffer with Christ; it is to me the highest honor to be conformed to his image. Unfruitful trees are, at length, cut down, and cast into the fire. I have within myself a certain sign, that I am a chosen tree in the garden of God. The Husbandman purgeth me, and causeth me to bring forth fruit meet for repentance. As the lancet draws the unhealthy blood from the veins, so does the cross extract the love of sin from the heart. What the fire is to the gold, and the polishing mill to the precious stone, that must I find in affliction. Affliction gives me light, that I may see God. Joseph was not known to his brethren when he treated them kindly, but when he assumed severity. Trials raise my heart to God. The more the waters of the deluge increased, the higher the ark mounted upwards. The myrrh of the cross preserves me from the corruption of sin; it is indeed bitter, but salutary. In the bitter and salt water they catch the great fish; in the fresh water, only the small. The greater the cross, the greater the saint. The wind must separate the wheat from the chaff, and the cross the righteous from the wicked. The ungodly abide not under the cross; they are as the chaff which the wind driveth away. The corn falls at the feet of the winnower; the righteous fall under the cross before God, and submit to his will. Such was Christ; "Father, not my will, but thine be done." Such, by his grace, will I also be. In affliction every one becomes known; whoever belongs to the Israel of God passes through the sea; whoever is numbered with the Egyptians, sinks as lead in the mighty waters. We must pass under the rod. If God chastise us not here as a Father, he will punish us there as a Judge.

I will kiss the rod of the Father, that I may escape the wrath of the Judge. My prayers to God shall be, not that I may be exempt from the cross, but that I may bear it patiently.

ON

THE NAME OF JESUS

THE world attempts much, partly in its own name, partly in another's name, partly even in the devil's name. I concur not in these attempts.

Whatever a man undertakes in his own name, must terminate in his disgrace. Without God, our wit ensnares, and our power confounds us.

Much less does that succeed which a man attempts in the name of another. Is he said to be *strong?* Yet he is only flesh, and will return to the dust. How powerful was Sennacherib! yet of what avail? Trust not in princes, they are but men. Today they bloom, to-morrow perish. Is he said to be *wise?* He may be wise to his own and my destruction, as Ahitophel—and who knows how long? Nebuchadnezzar was said to be wise, but not always.

Least of all does that succeed, on which a man ventures in the name of the devil. If Satan is with us, God is against us. Without God, without success,—I will not act thus.

Must no attempt then be made? Yes, if it be made in the name of Jesus. The name of Jesus is my comfort. It is as the balm to my wounded soul. "Thy name is as ointment poured forth," Sol. Song 1:3. Sin only can trouble me; Jesus only can delight me: for there is salvation in no other; neither is there any other name given among men, whereby we must be saved. The name of Jesus is my refuge in every time of need. "The name of the Lord is a strong tower, the righteous runneth into it, and is safe," Prov. 18:10. Does hell rage against me? Let it rage; I fly to the name of Jesus; I plead it in the prayer of faith, and say, "Hast thou not promised, Lord, that whatsoever I ask in thy name, that will thy Father give me? I ask then, holy Father, in the name of thy well-beloved Son, by the mystery of his holy incarnation, by his agony and bloody sweat, by his cross and passion, to deliver me from mine enemies. I ask thee to rescue thy oppressed child, who no where else can find deliverance." I am safe in the strong tower of the name of Jesus.

The name of Jesus is my boast, I will tell you against whom. 1. Against *sin*. For of Him bear all the prophets witness, that through his name, whosoever believeth on him, shall obtain forgiveness of sins, Acts 10:43. My name is that of sinner; my Savior's name is Jesus, because he saveth his people from their sins. Does sin boast over my name? I in my turn will also boast. The blood of Jesus Christ, the Son of God, cleanseth from all sin.

2. Against *Satan*. He comes against me in battle array like Goliath; I fear him not, but confidently oppose him, and say with David, "Thou comest against me with sword, and spear, and shield, but think not that thou canst alarm me; I come in the name of the living God, of Jesus, the Lord of hosts, who hath already bruised thy head; do thy worst." When, in faith, I utter the name of Jesus, Satan flees from me with fear and shame. Thus I put to flight the armies of the aliens.

3. He is my boast against *all my enemies*. How fearfully did Saul breathe out threatenings and slaughter against the disciples of Jesus! but when the Lord met him on the way to Damascus, and said from heaven, "Saul, Saul, why persecutest thou me? I am Jesus, whom thou persecutest: it is hard for thee to kick against the pricks," Acts 9:5; his heart sank within him, and he began to tremble and quake. O world, in the name of Jesus I will trample thee under foot. Thou persecutest not me, but Jesus in me. What canst thou, a powerless creature, effect against the Almighty God? Thou art but as the stubble before the whirlwind. If He be for me, who can be against me? The powers of hell cannot injure me. True, they may have death in league with them, but what then? Stone, burn, drown me, do what you may, I cry with Stephen, "Lord Jesus, receive my spirit," Acts 7:59. Do you not behold Jesus standing in the clouds at the right hand of God, and waiting for my soul? Set it free from this tabernacle; he will receive it into heaven. Can you pluck it out of the hands of Jesus? I fearlessly say to death, "Jesus is my life, and thou art my gain."

Beloved brother in Christ, dare all things in the name of Jesus: thou canst not fail. Amen.

ON WEAK FAITH

EVEN in a spark there is fire. Only try it, lay suitable fuel on it, and see whether it will not kindle the heap, and burst into a flame. Faith, though it may be weak, is nevertheless faith. Faith is not always a glowing torch, it is sometimes a glimmering taper. The taper gives light, as well as the torch, but not so brightly.

Faith is the eye by which we look to Jesus. A dim-sighted eye is still an eye; a weeping eye is still an eye. You sit in tears and say, How fearful this unbelief! oh! that I had faith. But, beloved, he really believes, who heartily bewails his supposed unbelief; for such tears demonstrate the desire after faith. And he who desires to believe, is declared by the word of God to have faith. It is God who puts into our hearts the good desire, as well as brings the same to good effect; and, therefore, he will not disdain the one more than the other.

Faith is the hand with which we lay hold of Jesus. A trembling hand is still a hand. And he is a believer, whose heart within him trembles when he touches but the hem of the Savior's garment, that he may be healed. You frequently exclaim, "Oh, how can I derive comfort from the wounds of Jesus! I shudder when I reflect on the greatness of my sins, I am a stranger to peace;"—yet to have stretched forth the hand to Jesus, this also is faith. Say, "Lord, increase my faith."

Faith is the tongue by which we taste how good the Lord is. A feverish tongue is nevertheless a tongue. And even then we may believe, when we are without the smallest portion of comfort; for our faith is founded, not upon feelings, but upon the promises of God.

Faith is the foot by which we go to Jesus. A lame foot is still a foot. He who comes slowly, nevertheless comes. A Christian must in his faith, look, not at the manner, but the object. What does your faith apprehend? The Savior. How does it apprehend him? With much weakness. Let not that distress you, if only it apprehend Him. God bestows salvation, not because of your act, but on account of the object of your faith, which is Christ. There are two hands which lift me up to heaven. My hand of faith lays hold of Jesus, and clings to his merits. The Lord's hand of grace, lays hold of me, and comes to my help. It is sufficient for me, and his strength is made perfect in my weakness. My hold is easily separated; His is immoveably secure. Thus, I am, at the same time, weak in myself, and strong in the Lord.

ON

THE IMMOVEABLE GROUND OF FAITH

"A THREEFOLD cord is not quickly broken," Eccles. 4:12. And such I possess. *God is good*, that rejoices me; *God is true*, that sustains me; *God is almighty*, that strengthens me. The goodness of God lays on me the cross; his truth enables me to bear it; and his power to overcome. Goodness, truth, and power alike succour me. The first is as the heart, the second as the mouth, and the third as the head. Having these in the Lord, what more do I require? His heart overflows with pity, his mouth utters words of the most tender love and consolation, and his hand can make all things new. Let the enemy approach and rage against me, God is full of goodness; let him threaten me, God is faithful, and can comfort me; let him despoil me, or cast at me his fiery darts, God can enrich, and heal me by his grace. The enemy gives me not one word of consolation in distress; the grace of God administers it abundantly. The world is ever changing and fluctuating in opinion. My God abideth the same forever. The world is false and deceptive, who can trust in it? God hath promised, and will also perform. The world possesses but little power. God's hand is not shortened that it cannot save. I will trust in Him, and not be afraid; for my confidence is founded on his grace, his faithfulness, and power in Christ Jesus. Blessed is the man who trusteth in Him.

ON

THE TRUE CHRISTIAN

IF four things unite in you, then are you a true Christian, And what are they? Faith, life, suffering, and death. Faith constitutes, life manifests, sufferings prove, and death crowns the Christian. Faith lays the foundation, life builds upon that foundation, sufferings cement, and death perfects the building.

Faith takes hold of Jesus, and says, *Thou* art mine; what thou *art* is mine, what thou *hast*, all is mine. "Whom have I in heaven but thee? and there is none upon earth that I desire besides thee. My flesh and my heart faileth: but God is the strength of my heart, and my portion for ever," Psalm 73:25, 26.

In the Christian's *life*, love is especially prominent, therefore St. Paul exhorts us to "walk in love" Eph. 5:2. Love throws itself into the arms of Jesus, and says, "I am thine; whatsoever I am, that am I in thee, and all that I have is thine. To thee I live, to thee I die; living and dying I am thine."

Patience is a special grace of *suffering*, according to the admonition of St. Paul, "Be patient in suffering." Patience casts itself down at the feet of Jesus, and says, "I will bear the indignation of the Lord, because I have sinned against him," Micah 7:9. Lay on me, my Savior, what thou wilt, when thou wilt, how thou wilt, I will readily bear it. Let it be the cross, so that thou with it give me strength; strength to sustain it, strength to overcome. Thou art faithful, and sufferest no man to be tempted above that he is able, but makest a way to escape, that he may be able to bear it.

In *dying*, joy is a grace which claims peculiar eminence. It clings to the Savior, and exclaims, "Where thou art, I shall be also; and I am persuaded that neither death, nor life, shall be able to separate me from the love of God which is in Christ Jesus my Lord," Rom. 8:38, 39.

I will, through the grace of God, use all diligence, that I may rightly believe, faithfully live, patiently suffer, and joyfully die. Then shall I bear the marks of a true Christian, and His shall be the glory.

ON

THE EXCELLENCY OF DIVINE GRACE

WE are often careful and troubled about many things, but about the "one thing needful" we are, comparatively, unconcerned, Luke 10:42.

Some desire to be rich, and they would indeed be rich had they learned to be satisfied. "Godliness with contentment is great gain," 1 Tim. 6:6.

Others weary themselves to attain earthly greatness, and they would certainly be great if they could acquire self-control. "He that is slow to anger is better than the mighty; and he that ruleth his spirit than he that taketh a city," Prov. 16:32.

Multitudes eagerly engage in the pursuit of pleasure, and it would not elude their grasp, if they had learned so to live that they might not fear to die. But who is mindful of that which makes for his peace? To be reconciled to God, and partake of his saving grace, is our supreme good. For this one thing will I strive. A gracious God is riches enough for me. In his grace I have full contentment and great gain. Nor do I wish for higher honor than I already possess in being called a child of God, and his own inheritance. I desire no other happiness. Why do men inquire so little after grace? Is it not because they do not seek that of which they are ignorant? Few know God in his goodness; few taste and see how gracious he is. Ask of God that he would be pleased to shed his grace into your heart, which may cause you to thirst after him, as the hart panteth after the water-brooks. But how can God dwell in a heart which will not forsake its sin? There is no affinity between the comforts of God, and those of the world. "If any man love the world, the love of the Father is not in him," 1 John 2:15. It is not till the world has become bitter to us, that we learn rightly to value the loving-kindness of the Lord. "He hath filled the hungry with good things; and the rich he hath sent empty away," Luke 1:53.

ON THE

ESTIMATE WHICH IS FORMED OF THE BELIEVER

"As deceivers, and yet true," 2 Cor. 6:8. Such was the description of the early followers of Jesus. Their Savior had been reviled before them. And how has it been with his servants of a later age? I will inform you. Athanasius, Luther, Arndt, and others of the same character, were eminent in gifts and Christian graces; but what was their motto? Was it not, "As deceivers, and yet true?" True before God and his people; deceivers in the estimation of men. What did Caiaphas and the rulers think of Christ? That he was a Samaritan and a deceiver. What did Nicodemus, Joseph of Arimathea, and other holy men esteem him? As true. You live in accordance with the gospel, and follow Christ in the exercise of saving faith; the children of God acknowledge in you the power of the truth, and give God the glory. But what say the Pharisees? "He is a heretic, a deceiver, and troubler of the people." Such men put hitter for sweet, and sweet for bitter; they put darkness for light, and light for darkness. And what marvel? for he who can rightly appreciate the religion of Jesus must love it; and he who loves it, must know it; and he who knows it, must he taught by the Spirit of God. The natural man cannot form a more correct judgment of the doctrine of Christ, than a blind man can of colors. How can he have light and grace from heaven, who, blinded by the prince of darkness, hates and persecutes the Savior in his people? How can light and darkness, Christ and Belial, God and Satan, dwell in the same heart? Let it not distress you, if those who know not Jesus should charge you with being a heretic and a deceiver. They drink up iniquity like water, and their hearts cast forth wickedness as an overflowing well. The gospel, which to others is a savor of life unto life, is to them a savour of death unto death. Vain in their imaginations, and their foolish heart darkened, they have become hardened like Pharaoh. Whilst we pity them, and commend them to God, we need not fear their criminations; but let us ever seek to approve ourselves in the sight of Him who searcheth the hearts, and trieth the reins of the children of men, Jer. 17:10.

MARY AND MARTHA; OR, FAITH AND LOVE

BE not solicitous about solitude or society. Mary sits in calmness and composure at the feet of Jesus. Martha is employed in active service, and is careful about many things. I speak of faith and love. They are sisters, and dwell together, yet they differ in their characters and occupations. Faith is Mary, "exalted" in heavenly contemplations and devotions, and "bitter" in her hatred of that which is carnal and sinful: she sits with delight at the feet of Jesus in deepest humility, and hears his word. Love is Martha, who receives Jesus into her house, desirous to supply his necessities, and those of his disciples, not only liberally, but with every mark of honor; and she invites her sister to participate in her labor. "Lord," she says, "dost thou not care that my sister hath left me to serve alone? bid her therefore that she help me," Luke 10:40. Jesus is the arbitrator, and whilst he suggests an important caution, he confirms them in the faithful discharge of their respective duties: "Martha, Martha," he says, "thou art careful and troubled about many things: but one thing is needful: and Mary hath chosen that good part, which shall not be taken away from her," ver. 41, 42. Both must continue, faith and love. Mary must hear the word of Jesus; Martha must serve him. Mary must receive; Martha must give; but Mary must have the pre-eminence.

Let your first care be for yourself, then for your neighbor. You must be made a partaker of heavenly blessings before you can dispense them to others. If there be no tree, how can there be fruits? "Walk in love," saith St. Paul, "as Christ hath loved us," Eph. 5:2; and St. John, "We love him, because he first loved us," 1 John 4:19. Our love is like a taper, which must be lighted by the fire of Divine love. The love of Christ must first penetrate our heart, and then can we communicate to our neighbor of that which we have already received from Him. Jesus hath fed us with the bread of life, and given us to drink of living water, and clothed us with the garments of salvation: then it is that we can feed and clothe his hungry and thirsty and naked people; and, inasmuch as we do it to one of the least of these, his brethren, we do it unto him.

There is no true faith without good works, as there is no living body without motion. As the love of Jesus is apprehended by faith, so doth it urge men to do their utmost for his glory. When the corn is sown in the field, it remains not long hidden from our sight, but springs forth, and manifests itself in the fruits which it produces.

And as there is no true faith without good works, so can there be no good works without faith; for the word of God implants it: and faith is the root of good works, which are the exhibition and manifestation of that very word, in the life and conduct of a believer.

These three things are united together, as with a golden chain,—the word, faith, and works. The word is the seed of faith; and to faith, in its turn, are good works to be attributed. But faith and works are different from each other, and have respect to different objects. By the former, we apprehend the righteousness of Christ, for our justification; by the latter, we manifest our union with Christ, and evidence the sincerity and depth of our love to him. The one has reference to God, the other to our neighbor.

Let your care extend to both. Seek faith, that you may obtain salvation; be diligent in good works, that you may evidence your faith both to yourself and others, and give glory to God.

ON THE

THREE CARDINAL VIRTUES

WHEN Jesus endured his bitterest agony in the garden of Gethsemane, he suffered Peter, and James, and John only to be present. When, also, on the mountain of the transfiguration he manifested his Divine glory, they alone of all his disciples were privileged to be with him. And why these three *only?* Was it not because they were the most beloved? Peter, as the first-born of the apostles, who continually was near him. John, as the disciple whom he loved, and who should zealously defend his Godhead against the heretics Ebion and Cerinthus, and say, "We beheld his glory, the glory as of the only begotten of the Father, full of grace and truth," John 1:14. James, as he who should be the first martyr of the apostles. The more beloved, the nearer to suffering; for those whose hearts are united, participate in each other's sorrows. The more beloved, the nearer also to joy; because those who suffer with Christ shall partake richly of his consolations. He who knows not sorrow is destitute of joy. We must bear a cross in following Jesus. Think not to be exempted from it.

Do you ask yet again, why especially these three, Peter, James, and John? Let St. Paul answer. "Now," saith he, "abideth faith, hope, charity, these three," 1 Cor. 13:13. By the three names of these apostles, these cardinal virtues are expressed. Peter is termed a "rock," and appropriately, since by his faith and knowledge of the truth he built upon Jesus, the Rock of our salvation. James signifies, "he that tramples under foot," and justly, since he trampled even Satan himself beneath his feet when he loved not his life, even unto death. John expresses the grace, gift, or mercy of God; and his great theme was the love of God, even till his death. Peter represents *faith*, which rests upon Jesus, the tried Cornerstone, and sure Foundation, and cries, "Here I am safe; the gates of hell cannot prevail against me." James furnishes an emblem of *hope*, which superior to all earthly things, looks heaven-ward and exclaims, "All things I esteem as dross, that I may win Christ." Joyful through hope, heaven will afford us better things than these. In John we behold charity, or *love*, which delights to be near to Jesus, and says, "I am thine, and thou art mine; nothing shall divide us."

Faith, hope, and love are with Jesus during his agony and bloody sweat in the garden of Gethsemane. Faith says, "In blood is my increase." Hope, "After the conflict the crown." Love, "I am not better than my Savior; I will suffer with him, that we may be glorified together." Faith exclaims, "Jesus dwells with me. The house may be stormed, but he will keep it in safety." Hope adds, "My security is in Jesus; he is the anchor of my soul, both sure and steadfast." Love, "I cling to my Savior; by his grace enabling me, I will never leave him nor forsake him."

Faith, hope, and love ascend with Jesus the hill of Tabor, to behold his transfiguration. We are not always in tears. "Weeping may endure for a night, but joy cometh in the morning," Ps. 30:5. God lifteth us up, as well as casteth us down. The burden and heat of the day are succeeded by rest and refreshment. Faith, be not weak, you have Jesus near you, and he will give you to drink out of the river of his pleasures. He is the chief among ten thousand, the altogether lovely, Sol. Song, 5:10. It is good to be here. Hope, do not fluctuate; you "look for the Savior, the Lord Jesus Christ: who shall change our vile body, that it may be fashioned like unto his glorious body, according to the working whereby he is able even to subdue all things to himself," Phil. 3:20, 21. In what manner do you behold the Savior in his glory on the mount of the transfiguration? His countenance shineth like the sun, and he is the Sun of righteousness; his garment is white and glistering, so that no fuller on earth could whiten it; he is pure and holy, and he washes us that we may be whiter than snow. Be of good courage; the time will come when you who believe in Jesus, and are as a despised taper in the estimation of the proud, shall shine as the brightness of the firmament, and as the stars, for ever and ever. The time is not distant when in your glorified bodies, before the throne, you shall be clothed in white robes, with palms in your hands.

Be therefore joyful in hope. "The night is far spent, the day is at hand," Rom. 13:12. The morning will ere long break, and the shadows flee away. Let not love be cold. Go but to the hill of Tabor. There Jesus will open to you his heart. His purposes are gracious when he leadeth you to suffering and to sorrow. He loveth you with an everlasting love, with a love stronger than death. He is your salvation, your heaven, your all. In possessing him, everlasting joy and gladness is your portion. "In his presence is fullness of joy; at his right hand there are pleasures for evermore," Psa. 16:11.

ON LITTLE SINS

LITTLE dogs often inflict the greatest injury.

The stag does not think so; and yet, at length, he becomes conscious of the fact by the injuries he receives. He holds at bay the great hounds, disables them, and dashes them against the tree; the little dogs, in the meantime, rush in upon him in multitudes, and tear pieces of flesh from his body: he heeds not the wounds till they fester and mortify, and then he dies.

You guard against great sins; you would not be thought to be a murderer, a thief, an adulterer, lest you should be put to shame before the world; in the meantime, the flesh tempts you to little sins, of which you are not aware. You love the society of the world, and adopt its customs; thus, unobserved, your soul is wounded; you are not conscious of the wound; your former zeal imperceptibly diminishes, and becomes extinguished, and, at length, you perish of your wounds. See how thus little sins are often the source of more evil than great ones; for great sins you consider to be such, and avoid, but little sins you think not to be sins, and are not on your guard against them. I counsel you to deem no sins little. However small they appear to you, they are displeasing to God; they wound the conscience; they become the root of many greater sins. "Behold, how great a matter a little fire kindleth!" James 3:5. Throw a stone in a lake, and it makes many circles, every one larger than the preceding; for if one be made, it is the cause of another which is greater, and that again is succeeded by another yet greater still; and thus it is with regard to sin. A little one is the origin of a great one, which, in its turn, gives birth to a greater. And, therefore, it has been well said by St. Bernard, "A heart that is given to God keeps itself from little, as well as from great sins, since those who commit great sins, usually begin with little. There is not a single sin, be it ever so little, which does not deserve death. For "the wages of sin is death," Rom. 6:23, and if a man should keep the whole law, with the exception of sinning in one point, he would be guilty of all, James 2:10. Augustine places the same truth before us when he says, "Esteem no sins as small, because they are small; but fear because they are many. How small are the grains of sand, but if too many be put into a ship she will sink! and how small are the drops of rain, yet they cause the rivers to overflow, and sweep away the habitations of man!"

To avoid and to fly from little sins, is a sign of an enlightened soul. For, as in the light of the sun even the smallest particle of dust may be seen, whilst men in darkness cannot perceive an accumulated heap; thus, the more a man is enlightened from on high, the more quick is his apprehension of that which is evil, and the more intense his hatred of it.

I will regard as sins all things which are opposed to God, however small they may appear; no sin is too small to condemn me, if God did not extend to me his grace.

ON

THE HOUR OF NEED

ALL things are lost, I cannot but despair! No, my soul, God may yet send deliverance. When the earth is silent, then do the heavens answer; when vain is the help of man, then the help of God is nearest at hand. Save, Lord, for the water goeth over my soul.

At the marriage in Cana of Galilee, the Virgin Mary supposed that Jesus would not suffer a total want first to be apparent, but would miraculously supply wine while some of the stock of the house yet remained. But Jesus thought otherwise and replied, "Mine hour is not yet come," John 2:4. The utmost extremity is the time of deliverance. The sisters of Lazarus thought that if Jesus had been with them, their brother had not died, but that when he was dead, there was no remedy; yet the Lord made it manifest to the contrary, by raising him from the dead. "In the mount the Lord shall be seen." When the eyes of Hezekiah are closing in death; when the woman of Capernaum has spent all her substance upon physicians; when the widow of Nain is conveying her son through the gate of the city; then Jesus draws near, and shows that he only can help when all other means fail.

You say, "Thank God, I have some provisions left; my need is not yet so very great." It is well; as yet Jesus has nothing to do for you, since your wants are already supplied. But a time of great trial arrives; your necessities are apparent; you are disquieted, and cry, "If help be not soon sent, we all shall be lost; we must perish." But wait only a little till you have nothing more left, then Jesus will appear to your aid.

Did he not make all things from nothing? He has still the same power, and puts it forth in your behalf. In the wilderness God doeth wonders; thus he rains manna upon us out of heaven, and causes the water to flow from the stony rock; there an angel points out a well, and ravens bring bread and flesh to the servant of the Lord; there Jesus satisfieth five thousand men with five loaves; and twelve baskets full of fragments, that remained over and above to them that had eaten, are collected by his disciples. When all around you is waste and desolate, your means of subsistence gone, and in deep distress you cry, "Whence shall I obtain bread in the wilderness, that I and my children may eat?" then God will give you bread. Either it will descend from heaven, or an angel will convey it to you, or even hunger itself shall be made to nourish you instead of bread. Marvel not at what I say. God is daily doing wonders. But if you believe not, there shall not be an accomplishment of these things to you. The hand of God meets our hand of faith, and gives to it the blessing. Oh that you would trust God to provide for you! His storehouse is always furnished with bread, and his fountain of water is full. When the floods overflow me, then he draweth me out of the deep waters. Wait only for the right time. The hour of Mary was made to accord with that of Jesus, and not the hour of Jesus with hers. Your extremity must become known to others, that God may receive honor in your deliverance. Why so impatient? "He that believeth shall not make haste," Isa. 28:16. God tarrieth not, whatever you may think. His purposes are hastening to their accomplishment. In infinite wisdom he will then work, when his hour is come; and that is the time of our greatest need. Hear the language of David, "It is time for thee, Lord, to work: for they have made void thy Law," Psa. 119:126; and thus saith the Lord by the mouth of the prophet Isaiah, "Now will I arise; now will I be exalted; now will I lift up myself." And why now? because the utmost distress and misery prevail; because "the earth mourneth and languisheth: Lebanon is ashamed, and hewn down: Sharon is like a wilderness; and Bashan and Carmel shake off their fruits," Isa. 33:9, 10.

Whatever may occur, I will never doubt God's almighty power, but say, Lord, keep me; thy right hand can make all things new. He forsaketh not his child whom he enableth to trust in him—I know it.

ON

THE USE OF MEANS

THE means which God appoints we must not despise, nor yet must we rest in them; but, whilst using them, we should look up to God for his blessing that they may prosper. A little bread sustains me, but it is through the blessing of God. A little medicine heals me, a fragrant flower refreshes me, but it is from the same cause. A dear friend comforts me; the comfort can continue only by the Divine blessing. Mine eye must, therefore, be directed to Him from whom cometh my help. The ungodly, who only look to the means, and not to God, make an idol of the means. As often as you take a piece of bread between your lips, and believe not that it is God who gives it the power of satisfying hunger, you make the bread your god. If you have bread, you have confidence, for your god still exists; if you are destitute of bread, you are confounded, because the god who fed you is no more.

I will use the means which God appoints, that I may not tempt him; yet I will not trust in the means, lest I should deny Him. God can easily help us without the means, for he has power to do so. It was neither herb nor mollifying plaster, that restored them to health, but thy word, O Lord, which healeth all things, Wisdom 16:12. But means can be of no avail without God; they are utterly powerless. When God withholds his blessing, they shall eat and not be satisfied, Hosea 4:10. Wait ever on the Lord, and all shall be well.

ON THE

FRUIT OF THE WORD OF GOD

"A GREAT outlay, but small return." So saith the husbandman, after he has sown much corn in his land, but reaped only a bad crop. If you are similarly circumstanced, how loud is your complaint. And has not God good reason to mourn over you, who every year are privileged to hear so many sermons, and yet with so little improvement? In the midst of such bright light to walk in Egyptian darkness, how can this be pleasing to Him? The earth receives the seed in vain, if it yields no increase. And you hear the word of God to no good purpose, if you receive it not in faith, for your comfort, and if it influence not your lives. It is indeed no small proof of the long-suffering of God, that he permits His word to dwell among us so richly, when we so shamefully abuse it. Where shall we find such patience in a husbandman? When he has sown his field two or three years without increase, will he entrust his seed to it again? But God has not ceased during your whole life to continue his word to you, whether you remain without benefit from it, or become even worse than you were before. Doubtless, the intercession of Christ moves him to this wondrous forbearance. We have an illustration of this, in the gospel of St. Luke. When the owner of the vineyard said, "Behold, these three years I come seeking fruit on this fig-tree, and find none: cut it down; why cumbereth it the ground?" the dresser of the vineyard answered him and said, "Lord, let it alone this year also, till I shall dig about it, and dung it: and if it bear fruit, well: and if not, then after that thou shalt cut it down," Luke 13:7–9. You see here how God seeks the spiritual good of men; you see also his long-suffering, that he willeth not the death of sinners, but that they should turn unto him, and live: but when justice seems to demand their rejection, the intercession of Christ prolongs the day of grace. And I doubt not that there are those on earth, who having the good of souls deeply at heart, cry day and night earnestly on their knees, that God would spare some one dear to them a little longer, and they would entreat him with tears to turn unto the Lord, and it might be, that by grace, he would be gained, and bear fruit. Such prayers of his servants, God graciously hears, and replaces the sword in its scabbard, to give them yet further time to repent. He would rather spare than punish, since he is goodness itself. Happy are the places where such Christians dwell; but beware, my friend, that thou despise not the riches of His goodness, and forbearance, and long-suffering, not knowing that the goodness of God leadeth thee to repentance. As ambassadors for Christ, we beseech you that you receive not the grace of God in vain. "Behold, now is the accepted time: behold, now is the day of salvation," 2 Cor. 6:2. God will, at length, cut down the unfruitful tree; he will be weary of sparing. Oh, seek his grace, and that right early. May He vouchsafe, in mercy, that we be filled with the fruits of righteousness, through Jesus Christ, to the praise of the glory of his grace! Amen.

ON

THE RIGHT USE OF TIME

"LORD, this time is mine, and thine," sang a certain nun. It may be so. I adopt her language, "Lord, this time is mine, and thine." The world is shut out; shall I serve it? I have no leisure. The time is mine, and my God's. What is more transitory than time? and its end is eternity. If, through grace, I redeem it, an eternity of blessedness is beyond; if otherwise, of misery. If I serve God, I shall dwell forever in heaven; if the world, in hell. Do you know what especially distresses me? It is, that I have so many hours taken from my God, and wasted in the service of the world. Oh, that I could redeem them with burning tears! Silver and gold have I none. But hear again. The sentiment expressed by the nun is not good. The time is not mine, but my God's; not a moment continues in my hand. Shall I serve the world today? The day is his. "Today if ye will hear his voice, harden not your hearts," Heb. 3:7, 8. Will you wait till to-morrow? Who knows where I shall be on the morrow? Today I walk on the earth: to-morrow the earth may cover me. However patiently the world might wait, yet I should grudge it even an hour. Every day belongs to my God. "Exhort one another daily, while it is called Today; lest any of you be hardened through the deceitfulness of sin," Heb. 3:13.

O world! the time is not mine. I cannot serve thee. What saith my God? I appeal to him; for, without his permission, I dare not.

ON PRAYER

"Is any among you afflicted? let him pray," Jas. 5:13. Ask Hezekiah what I should do when worn down by sickness. He will answer, Pray. Ask Jonah what is his advice when my soul is agitated with anxiety and alarm; he will exclaim, Pray. Ask David how I shall find consolation for my fainting soul, when I am oppressed with sorrow; and his reply you will find in Psa. 42:4, 7–9, "When I remember these things, I pour out my soul in me. All thy waves and thy billows are gone over me. Yet the Lord will command his loving-kindness in the daytime, and in the night his song shall be with me, and my prayer unto the God of my life. I will say unto God my rock, Why hast thou forgotten me? why go I mourning because of the oppression of the enemy?"

It is not pleasing to God that we pine under our afflictions, and vex our souls; nor is it of any avail. We should rather pray, and spread before him all our troubles. It is true, that He who knoweth all things is well acquainted with our state. He who numbers the drops of rain, and the sands on the sea-shore, counts also our tears. How should He not be fully aware of our circumstances! Hath he not himself sent the trial? and doth he not help us to bear it? He saw the oppression of the children of Israel in Egypt; and he beholdeth also my distress, and perceiveth my trouble. Nevertheless, it is his will that we should cry unto him for deliverance. He will be inquired of for these things; and by the act of prayer, will the spirit of prayer be more excited within us. The more fuel a man heaps upon the fire, the brighter it will burn. By means of prayer, we manifest our confidence in God; for to no one will a man disburden his heart, but to a friend in whom he can trust. By prayer we remove a heavy load from the mind. God taketh no delight in our misery, but in our good, and therefore calleth upon us to confess our sins, and make known our requests, that he may confer the blessings of his grace. Prayer moves the God of heaven to come to our help. When we open our wounds before him, he will not fail to apply the remedy.

But who is he, you inquire, that can pray? My brother, as God is wont especially to administer comfort when you are utterly destitute and forlorn; so you pray most earnestly when you think, that for anguish you have not the power to utter a prayer. Not to be able to pray, and yet to desire to pray, constitutes the most earnest supplication. "The Spirit also helpeth our infirmities: for we know not what we should pray for as we ought: but the Spirit itself maketh intercession for us with groanings which cannot be uttered," Rom. 8:26. If I cannot pray, I will yet sigh; if I cannot sigh, I will yet think of God. If I cannot think of God, he will yet think of me, and graciously behold the anguish of my soul. He will fulfil my desire; I confidently believe it.

I AM A CHRISTIAN

GET thee hence, Satan! I am a Christian. The vows of God are upon me. He is mine; I am his. You have nothing in me; not a hair of my head is yours; not a drop of my blood. I belong to Jesus. "You have no authority over a Christian," said the dying St. Martin to the wicked one, when he pressed upon him with his fiery darts.

Away, vain world! I am a Christian. Whatever you can give me, do I not already possess greater excellence in my Savior; and whatever you can take away, do I not still retain in Him? You cannot pluck *me* out of His hand, nor *Him* out of my heart.

Hence, sin! I am a Christian. The man indeed you can condemn, but not the Christian, since there is no condemnation to them who are in Christ Jesus, Rom. 8:1. If you are against me, Christ is for me—Christ who saveth his people from their sins; He who was made sin for us, that we might be made the righteousness of God in Him. Who shall lay anything to the charge of God's elect? God is with me who justifies. Who is he that condemneth? Christ has died for me; yea, rather risen again, who is ever at the right hand of God, who also maketh intercession for me, Rom. 8:33, 34. Christ is my Rock, and therefore the gates of hell cannot prevail against me; but whosoever striketh against this Rock shall stumble and fall.

Afflictions cannot harm me. "I am a Christian!" cried that tender virgin, the blessed Blandina, in the extremity of her suffering; and confessed that as often as she uttered these words, new strength was administered to her, and she was not sensible of pain. Christ who dwelleth in me, is my life, and his strength is made perfect in my weakness. "I suffer as a Christian," said the holy martyr Felicitas. I am indeed blessed if I suffer for righteousness' sake. He that suffers with Christ, will also with Him be glorified.

Poverty cannot discourage me. I am the purchased possession of my Savior. Doth he care for the worms which he hath created, how much more will he regard the souls for whom he hath shed his most precious blood?

Death cannot scare me. Christ is my life; to die is gain. I know full well that neither death nor life can separate me from the love of God, which is in Christ Jesus my Lord. In Christ I am well pleasing to my heavenly Father,—"accepted in the Beloved," Eph. 1:6. The world, it is true, loveth me not, but this gives me little concern, if only I am beloved by my heavenly Father. As a Christian, not in name only, but in reality, I am united to Christ by a living faith. He bears my sin and weakness, my curse and death, and gives me his righteousness and strength, his blessing and life. In Him I have all things; what then can I want? I am a Christian, and therefore must I suffer; no rose without a thorn, no sea without waves, no sky without clouds, no Christian without the cross: but what I Suffer, I suffer in him; and he is touched with a feeling of my infirmities. Shortly, in his own good time, he will take me hence, and I shall enter into his joy.

ON THE

LOVE OF GOD IN THE CROSS

WHATSOEVER God doeth is good, for "God is love," 1 John 4:8; and "Love worketh no ill to his neighbor," Rom. 13:10. You complain in your distress that God dealeth severely with you; that your case is worse than that of others. Take heed that you sin not against God. You say not that fire maketh you cold; you deny not that water communicates moisture; you declare not that the sun is the source of darkness. You charge God foolishly, when you ascribe to his displeasure the cross which he sends you. Is not God essentially love? Are you not, in Christ, so closely united with him, as to be one spirit? so indissolubly one, that, in Christ, God and man cannot be divided? Is not the relationship as intimate as that of the child with its parent, or the wife with her husband? And "love worketh no ill to his neighbor." If you, who are evil, can do no evil to your neighbor whom you love, how much less will God, who is goodness itself, do evil to man, whom he loveth, in Christ, as himself? Nevertheless, you say, suffering is hard upon me; but is it therefore evil? Oh no, but rather good and profitable for your soul. All things which are bitter to the flesh are not prejudicial to the soul. Love corrects, but it does not injure or spoil. Does the father act amiss when he uses the rod? Does the physician intend harm when he administers a bitter draught? As a silly child, or a self-willed patient, you would refuse the salutary discipline. You know not what benefits and blessings are concealed by the cross, and that God is correcting you that you may not perish with the world. David understood this matter much better. Hear how he speaks of it in Psa. 116:3. "The sorrows of death," he says, "compassed me, and the pains of hell gat hold upon me: I found trouble and sorrow." But did he regard this as a token of God's displeasure? Let him answer for himself. "What shall I render unto the Lord for all his benefits toward me? I will take the cup of salvation, and call upon the name of the Lord. I will pay my vows unto the Lord now in the presence of all his people. In the courts of the Lord's house, in the midst of thee, O Jerusalem. Praise ye the Lord," ver. 12, 14–19. You suppose that there is only anger and wrath in the cup which God giveth you to drink; but no, learn rather to esteem it, with David, the cup of love, "the cup of salvation." "All things work together for good to them that love God," Rom. 8:28. Should men devise evil against you, yet God will direct it to a good purpose, that his own honor and your spiritual good may thereby be promoted; and you may say to your enemies, as Joseph said to his brethren, "As for you, ye thought evil against me; but God meant it unto good," Gen. 50:20. He doth, indeed, for us, more and better than we can ask or think. He who hath done all things well, will not deny his own name. "Wait on the Lord: be of good courage, and he shall strengthen thine heart: wait, I say, on the Lord," Psa. 27:14.

ON THE

HELP OF GOD IN THE CROSS

WHEN help fails from the hills, it comes from the Lord. "Shall I lift up mine eyes to the hills? whence should my help come?" From them? Oh, no. "My help cometh from the Lord, which made heaven and earth," Psa. 121:1, 2: see the marginal reading.

We have need of help for the preservation of both soul and body; but whence shall it come? Our eyes direct us to the hills, they bid us trust in that which is great, strong, and powerful. On wealth; on the great ones of the earth; on princes, who are compared in the Scriptures to the hills. But all these hills must melt away like wax before the presence of the Lord of the whole earth. There is no hill that can afford us aid, if God contend with us. And if God be on our side, what need have we of men, who today are as hills, to-morrow as valleys; today rich, to-morrow poor; today alive, to-morrow dead? How can men help us when they cannot help themselves? Our help cometh from the Lord. When earth cannot benefit us, heaven will. "When my father and my mother forsake me, then the Lord will take me up," Psa. 27:10. Precious words! As good seed, made such by him, I shall be gathered into the garner; as poor, persecuted, and outcast, I shall be received beneath the shelter of his roof. The Hebrew, or rather the Talmudic word, which is rendered *foundling*, is derived from the root here used *to take up*. This then is the force of the passage before us. If dark clouds of affliction should arise, if the storm of calamity should sweep over me, if an ungodly world should pursue me, and cast me forth to be trampled underfoot, or swallowed up in the great waters, or torn by the wild beasts of the field; and if no one whatever should pity me as a foundling; yet I well know that God would deliver me from the terrors of the wicked, and take me up, and receive me into everlasting habitations, and hide me from the frowardness of the proud. In one word, let all forsake me, so that my God and Savior forsake me not. Let all cast me out, so that God receive me. I will seek no help from men. Should any man help me, he is only the instrument in the hand of God, for from God hath he first received, that he may give to me again. My help cometh from the Lord, and then especially is it manifest, when vain is the help of man. Earth, help thine own; God helpeth His own: he helpeth me, and I will praise his name forever.

ON

TRANQUILLITY BENEATH THE CROSS

"IN quietness and in confidence shall be your strength," Isa. 30:15. When Jesus was sailing with his disciples on the sea of Galilee, there suddenly arose a great storm, and the ship was covered with the foaming billows, and began to sink. The disciples in alarm cried out, "Lord, save us: we perish;" Matt. 8:25; but Jesus lay still, and slept.

Two persons often journey together in a little ship of the cross. One visitation overtakes both, yet they are not affected in the same manner. One curses, the other prays; one weeps, the other laughs; one complains, the other utters praise; one sinks, the other is saved. And what is the cause? One is an unbeliever, the other is a believer; the former has an evil, the latter a good conscience. One, therefore, is wakeful and restless; he would gladly drag the ship to land, or, at least, escape from it; the other is peaceful; he lives under the blessing of God, and with tokens of the Divine good pleasure; he says with David, "I will both lay me down in peace, and sleep: for thou, Lord, only makest me dwell in safety," Psa. 4:8.

A tranquil believer can, with Peter, sleep sweetly in prison, in the midst of his enemies. A man of the world, with an unquiet conscience, cannot take rest in a goodly mansion, though surrounded by his friends. The roses are not sufficiently soft for him: but the believer reposes peacefully upon thorns. Impatience makes a man pusillanimous; patience, magnanimous. The first is the parent of sorrow, fear, and disquietude; the second, of pleasure, security, and peace.

"In quietness and in confidence shall be your strength." If you would rest upon the billows as upon the solid rock, and enjoy peace in the midst of tribulation, then learn fully to acquiesce in the will of God. It is in vain that the storm beats against this wall, which remains fixed and immovable. The will of God shall be done, whether you will or not. Would it not be an act of folly in a man to bind his ship to a rock, and suppose that he could pull the rock towards him with the rope. He can only draw himself and his ship towards the rock. God will not bow to your will, you must bow to His. He is the Lord, you are the servant not of your will, but of His; and the will of God is better than yours. For God willeth not the death of a sinner, but that all men should come unto him and live, 2 Pet. 3:9; and for this purpose he frequently sendeth the cross. Do you obstruct the will of God, you obstruct your own salvation. Is not correction designed for the profit of children? He that refuses correction, refuses that which is most salutary. And what do you oppose? God doeth you no wrong. You deserve the scourge, and he useth only the rod. Is not this grace? Yield, then, to the discipline of your Father's hand. When God has conformed you to his will, then will your will be His, and this cannot be too soon.

Let the winds rage, and the billows lift up themselves on high; be thou still, and wait upon the Lord, and all shall be well. The proud waves of the sea must, at length, lay themselves to rest, and the sunshine shall succeed the storm.

ON

CHRISTIAN FORTITUDE

"VENTURE and win," so saith the world. The ungodly sinneth apace, he presumes upon God's mercy. In how much folly doth he indulge under the supposed convert of Divine grace! I hold not with him in his vain imaginations. He who sins against grace has wrath for his wages. He is guilty of a two-fold sin. Was it not enough to risk his soul? why should he, at the same time, set at naught the grace of God? Grace is not designed to screen, but to take away sin. Yet I nevertheless commend the motto of the world, "Venture and win." I approve not of a disheartened Christian. A Christian must fight; a warrior must possess courage. Without effort there is no success. Have I to contend with the world? Be it so. Where I have no advantage to expect, I have no loss to fear. You give me nothing, you take from me nothing: you have nothing, what can you bestow? I have nothing, of what can you deprive me? Whatever we have is of God. He gives to whom he will, and takes from whom he will: His name be praised.

Should Satan assault me, I heed him not. Great as is thy power, mine is greater. Art thou a lion? thou art in fetters; thou canst roar, but not devour. Art thou a dog? thou art chained; thou canst bark, but not bite. I may be opposed by multitudes of accursed spirits, but they that are with me are more than they that are against me. I fear not thousands of enemies that may encamp round about me. "They compassed me about like bees; they are quenched as the fire of thorns: for in the name of the Lord I will destroy them." Psa. 118:12. The enemy is full of wickedness; but why need I fear, since he cannot harm me. I am freed from his dominion and power. He is crafty, and he may do his worst. Wisdom is above cunning. I know Him, "in whom are hid all the treasures of wisdom and knowledge," Col. 2:3. He is of God made unto me wisdom, 1 Cor. 1:30.

Death may approach me with his terrors, but I welcome him as a friend. I know him well. I sit with him at the table, I see him in my chamber, I converse with him when apart from the society of man. I walk with him when I enjoy the pleasures of my garden; I am familiarized to death, since I die daily. Is death said to be bitter? I call him sweet. Is he said to be alarming? I call him pleasant. Is he said to be unwelcome? I hail his approach. Is he named death? I call him my life. Is he said to be inexorable? why then should I ask him to spare me? Of what can he deprive me? Of life? let him take it away. "Man at his best state is altogether vanity," Psa. 39:5. Of my body? I thank him for delivering me from the body of this death. Of what can he rob me that is mine? Is not God more to me than all things. In such a conflict great is my advantage. For rest I exchange toil and weariness; for sorrow I obtain joy. "To die is gain," Phil. 1:21.

Shall I also receive good at the hand of God? Yes, from Him above all. His dispensations may be dark, but his purposes are love. He correcteth with the rod of a father. "Behind a frowning providence he hides a smiling face." He comforts and embraces his weeping child, and, at length, crowns him with immortality and glory.

"I will not let thee go, except thou bless me," Gen. 32:26.

ON

THE WELL-BEING OF THE CHRISTIAN

IT is good to be here, where Jesus, Moses, and Elias pitch their tabernacle.

Jesus has his tabernacle in faith, for he dwells in our heart by faith. As Christ is pure, so the heart in which he dwells must also be pure. "Blessed are the pure in heart: for they shall see God," Mat. 5:8. Our hearts are purified through faith, which shows us the love of God, and the evil of sin, as an offence against Him, till the tears of godly sorrow fall from our eyes; it sprinkles the heart with the blood of Jesus Christ, his Son, which cleanseth us from all sin. It expels from the soul the world, and all worldly things, enabling us to perceive their bitterness; it manifests the sweetness of Jesus, and welcomes him to the heart, that there He may set up his throne.

The heart in which Jesus dwells must be adorned with love, gentleness, humility, and all other graces. The beauty of holiness must be conspicuous in the dwelling of the Savior. Would we be near Him, we must be like Him; and this transformation is the work of the Spirit in those that believe. "Beholding as in a glass the glory of the Lord, we are changed into the same image from glory to glory, even as by the Spirit of the Lord," 2 Cor. 3:18. Wherever Jesus is, it is good for us to be there. A believing heart is a happy heart; it is conformed to the will of Jesus. If I believe in Jesus, it must be well with me whatever I am called to suffer; for Jesus is mine, and all that he has is mine. In Him is only good; blessed be God. Do circumstances sometimes seem adverse to me, yet I know that all is well; for it is according to the will of Jesus, and His will is better than mine. Faith unites me to Jesus. Where he abides, there do I abide also. It is always good to be here.

Moses has his tabernacle in repentance. Wherever he finds sin, he denounces a curse; where repentance, a blessing. Whence does it arise that it is not well with you? You live in sin against your conscience. Sin separates you from God. Sin and the curse are as intimately related as daughter and mother. Would you escape the curse? repent, and forsake your sin. Let Moses hold up before you daily the mirror of the law, and show you yourself therein, that you may behold your guilt; let him touch your heart daily with the rod of God, that he may cause the tears of repentance to gush forth. Moses and Elias appear with Jesus, and speak to Him "of his decease which he should accomplish at Jerusalem" for our sins. Ask Moses where you can obtain salvation. He will answer, "Not in me, but in Jesus, for 'the Scripture hath concluded all under sin, that the promise by faith of Jesus Christ might be given to them that believe,' " Gal. 3:22. Ask Elias where salvation is to be found. He will point to Jesus and say, "To Him give all the prophets witness, that through his name whosoever believeth in Him shall receive remission of sins," Acts 10:43. Behold, then, Moses conducts you to Jesus, and it is good to be here. Moses casts down but to raise up; he kills to make alive; he throws you into the pit, that he may exalt you to the throne. "Godly sorrow worketh repentance unto salvation not to be repented of," 2 Cor. 8:10. Blessed is he that feareth the Lord.

Elias has his tabernacle in *prayer.* "Elias was a man subject to like passions as we are, and he prayed earnestly that it might not rain: and it rained not on the earth by the space of three years and six months. And he prayed again, and the heaven gave rain, and the earth brought forth her fruit," Jas. 5:17. The earnest prayer of faith must prevail. It is the key of heaven. Whenever I pray in the spirit, I open heaven, and take thence the blessings which I need.

You say, I want this or that; but can you not pray? A spiritual worshipper shall want nothing. Of what can he be destitute to whom the treasury of God is always open? Can you need any thing that you will not find there? Should the blessing not be received, the prayer of faith has not been offered up. God is more ready to give, than we are to ask. If we receive not, the fault is ours.

You speak of evils pressing upon you. Can you not pray? Every cross comes from heaven. When you pray under a cross, you shut or open heaven. If you shut heaven, the cross remains with you; if you open it, God sends from thence the showers of grace to comfort and refresh you, so that you may exclaim with grateful heart, "Thou sendest a plentiful rain upon thine inheritance, and refreshest it when it is weary," Psa. 68:2. Elias was indeed a great prophet, yet he was no holy angel, but only a man, with weaknesses and infirmities like ourselves. The grace which he received may be yours also. Ask what thou wilt, and it shall be done unto thee. In a word, believe, repent, pray, and the blessing of God shall ever rest upon you, and God shall be praised.

ON

REST IN GOD

IT is good to be here. Here is thine altar, O Lord of hosts. Here shall I be abundantly satisfied with the fatness of thine house, and thou shalt make me to drink of the river of thy pleasures, Psa. 36:8. Here is the foretaste of heaven. God in me, and I in him— this is indeed heaven. In the world I am the prey of anxiety; there my soul is like a timid bird, driven from its nest, deprived of its parents, or of its young; it lives in fear and solicitude, and knows not whither to fly. To whom shall I betake myself on earth? The world acts as though it knew me not. Whither then shall I go? I soar on high on the wings of desire, and pause not till I reach the altar of the Lord; there do I find rest. In Jesus alone I dwell in safety. In me, he saith, ye have peace, John 16:33. But will he reject me? By no means. He beckons you to himself, and says, Come, my dove, into the clefts of the rock. "Come unto me, all ye that labor and are heavy laden, and I will give you rest. Take my yoke upon you, and learn of me; for I am meek and lowly in heart: and ye shall find rest unto your souls," Matt. 12:28, 29. The dove of Noah found rest nowhere but in the ark. Am I out of Christ? I cannot find peace from the world, the flesh, or the devil. Do I hide myself in his wounds? Then I have a secure rest, which nothing can disturb. Doth the world rage? Let it rage; I am safe. Who can tear me from my Savior? The billows alarm me not; my ship is in the haven of rest. Have I tribulation in the world? My Savior leaves me not without comfort; the springs of joy are within me. My heart and my flesh rejoice in the living God. My Savior can administer richer joys than the world can cause trouble. This is my motto, "As sorrowful, yet always rejoicing," 2 Cor. 6:10.

Do my tears flow? Jesus wipeth them away from mine eyes. Doth the world persecute me, and expel me from my home, my city, or my country? What harm can it do when it drives me to the wounds of Jesus? It cannot deprive me of this refuge. Think of this, my soul, when thou desirest rest and safety. Seek them no where but in God. If you can find all things that you can desire in Him, why should you seek them elsewhere? Let it not distress you to be daily cast out by the world, that you may turn away your mind from beholding vanity, and seek your happiness in God. Delight in God more than countervails the bitterness of the world. Let one bitter drop fall into a cup of wine, and can you distinguish its flavor? You need not inquire as to the value of the joy that is in heaven; you may daily experience somewhat of it within your hearts, and sweeten with it all your sorrows. The heart of the believer is the rest and dwelling-place of God; there God manifests himself in his goodness.

"How amiable are thy tabernacles, O Lord of hosts! My soul longeth, yea, even fainteth for the courts of the Lord: my heart and my flesh crieth out for the living God," Psa. 84:1, 2. It is good, Lord, to be here—here will I build a tabernacle, and take my rest.

ON

GODLY SORROW AND THE PLEASURES OF THE WORLD

"PLEASURE here, and pleasure there," says one who would enjoy life in thoughtlessness. So also say I, but with a very different meaning. The world entices me with its pleasures; I regard them not. Whence do they arise?—from the flesh. Whither do they tend?—to death. They are, therefore, as distasteful to me as that to which they lead. Where are those who formerly lived in pleasure, and sang, "Come on, let us enjoy the good things that are present, and let us speedily use the creatures, like as in youth. Let us fill ourselves with costly wine, and let no flower of the spring pass by us. Let us crown ourselves with rosebuds, before they be withered. Let none of us go without his part of our voluptuousness. Let us leave tokens of our joyfulness in every place, for this is our portion, and our lot is this," Wisdom, 2:6–9. Where are these pleasure-takers now? It is with tears that I say it,

Unless they repented, they have all perished. How were the earthly gratifications of the rich fool exchanged for the pains of hell? I will choose that which cometh from heaven, and conducteth thither—"Godly sorrow" which worketh "repentance to salvation, not to be repented of," and not the "sorrow of the world," which "worketh death," 2 Cor. 7:10.

It is better to sorrow with God, than to be joyful with the world; better to weep with Jesus, than to laugh with the ungodly. No man by laughter will find Jesus. Where do you read that he laughed; but he is always near at hand to those that are in tears. Mary, the sister of Lazarus, wept; and Jesus wept with her. The pleasure of the world endeth in pain. "Woe unto you that laugh now! for ye shall mourn and weep," Luke 6:25. But the Christian's tears are succeeded by a harvest of joy. "They that sow in tears shall reap in joy. He that goeth forth and weepeth, bearing precious seed, shall doubtless come again with rejoicing, bringing his sheaves with him," Psa. 126:5, 6.

I find nothing upon earth that administers unmingled pleasure, but much to excite trouble. I look above, and behold my home, and Father's house, with joy; yet do I lament that I am not yet there, but am compelled to dwell longer in the land of Meshech, and among the tents of Kedar. I look beneath me, and tremble at the sight of hell. I look behind, and see the multitude of my sins crowding after me. I look before me, and cannot penetrate through the veil of the sorrows which await me. I look around me, and discover that I am on all sides beset by my deadly enemies. Wearied with the world, I look within, and, oh, what an abomination of desolation do I there behold! My tears flow apace; they chase each other down my cheeks; the deeper I penetrate, the more are the fountains of waters broken up.

But think not that I am destitute of joy. I have a God of grace who rejoices me; and in the midst of my pain, he enriches me with his secret consolations. I have the presence of my Savior, and the witness of his Spirit, and therein do I rejoice.

The pleasures of the world cease when troubles invade them; but mine continue beneath the heaviest cross. For never doth God manifest himself to me in greater sweetness than when, under visitations of trial, all things beside have been found to be bitter.

Let the world love its own, and live as it may, it has no pleasures for me. Through grace I have been taught the secret of peace.

ON

COMFORT IN AFFLICTION

I SAY under my trials, when they oppress me, "Whence come ye?" and the reply is, "From heaven," and I welcome them as the angels of God. I ask again, "Whither do ye conduct me?" and receive for answer, "To heaven." I hail, then, the chariots of fire, and horses of fire, as sent in mercy.

I marvel that afflictions so greatly distress men. But they do not rightly appreciate them. Many think that they proceed from beneath, or from the wickedness of men, and are not designed as blessings. But let the believer look upwards, and see the hand that strikes, and kiss the rod—it is the hand of a Father. Let him contemplate, also, the crown worn in heaven by them that came out of great tribulation, and have washed their robes, and made them white in the blood of the Lamb, and he will learn to bear his sorrows.

I "glory in tribulations," for I know who sent them—even my God, from whom can come nothing that is evil; my Creator, who would not destroy me; my Father, who desireth only the good of his child. I know what accompanies tribulations, the grace and blessing of God; and what want I more? Though not joyous now, but grievous, nevertheless they yield the peaceable fruits of righteousness to them that are exercised thereby, Heb. 12:11; their weight is refreshment; their sorrows are connected with the most cheering consolations. And I know that to which they lead—it is to heaven. They are a salutary means, in the hand of God, of preparing me for its enjoyment. I see beyond the cross, the crown—a crown of glory that fadeth not away.

"These things saith the First and the Last, which was dead and is alive. Fear none of those things which thou shalt suffer. Be thou faithful unto death, and I will give thee a crown of life," Rev. 2:8–10.

ON

THE COMMUNICATION OF SAVING GRACE

SIN is sweet at first, but bitter in the end. It is the precursor of suffering. The prodigal joyfully departed from his father's house, but he returned in sorrow. Think of the end. Grace is, for the most part, accompanied at first by pain, but succeeded by joy. It enters by the door of sincere repentance. Ask Hezekiah what was his experience, "Like a crane or a swallow," is his reply, "so did I chatter: I did mourn as a dove: mine eyes fail with looking upward," Isaiah 38:14. Ask David, and hear him exclaim, "Lord, make me to hear joy and gladness; that the bones which thou hast broken may rejoice," Psalm 51:8. Look at Mary Magdalen. Are not her eyes a fountain of tears? Behold the publican in the temple? Is not his heart oppressed with anguish as he cries out under the burden of his sins, "God be merciful to me a sinner?"

In worldly mirth man departeth from his God; in repentance he findeth God again, and his joy is often proportioned to the depth of sorrow which preceded. Hear the words of Hezekiah, "Behold, for peace I had great bitterness:" or, "when I looked only for peace, bitter, bitter was the portion which was given me to drink." But hear again his joyful exultation, "Thou hast in love to my soul delivered it from the pit of corruption: for thou hast cast all my sins behind thy back," Isa. 38:17. Hearken also to David, "I am weary with my groaning; all the night make I my bed to swim; I water my couch with my tears. Mine eye is consumed because of grief; it waxeth old because of all mine enemies," Psalm 6:6, 7. But soon his mourning is turned into gladness: "The Lord hath heard the voice of my weeping. The Lord hath heard my supplication; the Lord will receive my prayer," verses 8 and 9.

I had rather sow in tears and reap in joy, than sow in joy and reap in tears.

ON

LIVING UNTO THE LORD

WHEN the sun sets in the western sky, it rises in glory in another hemisphere. Thus is it with the child of God. The end of his mortal life is the beginning of immortality.

It is but a moment that we live. The remainder of our time is either past and irrecoverable, or is future and uncertain. The end of time is the beginning of eternity. Oh, think of eternity! Have you lived unto the Lord? then is your death not the end of your life, but the beginning. *You* do not die; your misery only dies, as said the martyr Cecilia. Through death you pass into a state better than that which you leave. You exchange weariness, trouble, and a transitory course, for rest, joy, and immortality. What have you lost? How great is your gain! Live so that you may die happy, and you will live so that you may die happy and you will live so that you shall never die.

This is the life of a Christian. God is the beginning, God is the end of all his works. He begins with prayer, he continues with thanksgiving. He cannot be idle. One work of faith and labor of love succeeds another to the end of his life. God is the source of his spiritual existence. To him tends his soul. It seeks not elsewhere for rest, but finds it abundantly in Him. The stone rests not in the air, but seeks its parent earth; nor can the soul find peace but in God.

ON

RENEWAL AFTER THE IMAGE OF GOD

"WHOSE is this image?" Matt. 22:20. It ought to be that of God. Your heart is a tablet, on which may he portrayed the image of God, of the world, or of the devil. That which you love most will he found thereon. If you love God, the image of God will he there; if the world, that of the world.

Love is a mirror by which the object is reflected. It is an evil token when that object is not God. Do you not recollect what Jesus said? "Render unto God the things that are God's." By the image which you bear, men know whose you are; and his whose you are in time, you will be throughout eternity. I will he wise in time, and seek that every lineament and feature of Jesus may be transferred to my soul. His doctrine and life shall be ever in my mind; and as I look unto him, and behold his glory, I trust I shall be "changed into the same image from glory to glory, even as by the Spirit of the Lord," 2 Cor. 3:18. Though there is in me much dissimilarity to my Lord, yet I will not desist from my endeavors, through his grace, to be conformed to him; nor will I doubt that I shall yet be made like him, for I shall see him as he is. He has left me an example, and goeth before me in the way, that I may walk in his steps. O blessed Jesus, take thou possession of my heart, that I may be new created in thine image and likeness, and may be thine both now and forever.

ON

THE KEEPING OF THE SOUL

THERE are many opinions among philosophers respecting the seat of the human soul. Some assign it to the heart; some again to the brain; whilst others affirm that it pervades the whole body. Without entering into curious speculations on this matter, we may in each of them trace the soul's operations. But beyond this, the Christian must learn to say with David, My life or "soul is continually in my hand," Psa. 119:109. That which is held in the hand is seen by the eye. You lead your child by the hand, or permit him to take hold of your arm, that he may not sustain injury. On the brief period of life depends an awful eternity. Let your soul be continually in your hand, that you may stand still every moment and consider its state. Is it inclined to that which is good? Ask Him who hath given the good desire, to bring the same to good effect Is it tempted to that which is evil? Recall to mind the shortness and uncertainty of life, and the utter worthlessness of all earthly things in comparison with the soul. Is your soul continually in your hand? You should have it ready to yield up always to the will of God. If you love God more than your life, then your life will remain to you in God, though you should immediately die; but if you love your life more than God, then will you lose both at once; and what is worse than all, you will yourself be lost forever. Here then you should keep your soul: but yet there is a more secure place. The hand of God can preserve it better than yours; therefore say with David, "Into thy hands, Lord, I commit my spirit," Psa. 31:5.

Luther often said, "I do not wish that my soul should be kept in my hand. If it were, Satan would long ago have seized it as his prey; but out of the hand of God, into which I have committed my soul, neither men nor devils can ever pluck it. It is the word of the Lord himself, 'My sheep hear my voice, and I know them, and they follow me: and no man is able to pluck them out of my Father's hand,' " John 10:27, 29.

ON

PEACE WITH GOD

PEACE in the midst of conflict—is it possible? It certainly is. I am always, and yet never at peace. You say there is peace, but take heed, the enemy is near at hand. I say, on the other hand, men and devils are in league against me; they encircle me around, and encompass me in on every side,—and yet I have peace. War without, peace within. My enemies are numerous; I fear not for their multitude. The danger is great; yet I am in safety. The enemy rage; the more their violence, the more courageously am I enabled to face them. You ask how this can be? I will inform you. Satan cannot rob me of my peace, though he devises one mischief after another. I desire not peace with him, for then it would be ill with me, for he has no peace with any but his friends: the peace, therefore, I have, I must possess, notwithstanding the violence of his rage against me. Christ gives me peace, comforts my heart, relieves me from fear and alarm, and raises me above the dread of all my enemies. This is the peace of God which keepeth the heart and mind in Jesus Christ, and passeth all understanding. In the midst of danger, it gives security; in weakness it affords the greatest power and strength; and makes me rich and content in poverty and want. It attracts the soul to Christ that it may taste his sweetness, and the more it knows of Christ, the more doth it cleave to him, till in him, as in a strong tower, it finds safety and rest. And what power can drive it thence? Not only doth Jesus keep the heart safe, but also joyful; and not only joyful, but courageous; yea, more than conqueror, and fearless of all enemies. I will in all things cheerfully acquiesce in the will of my gracious God and Father, so shall I enjoy peace in the midst of trouble.

ON

THE TRUE CHRISTIAN

ALL, and yet nothing—this is *the description of man.*

He is *all* since he is a brief epitome of all creatures, and has something in common with all. With the stone he has this in common, that he is a substance; with the trees and plants, that he grows and increases; with the dumb animals, that he possesses consciousness, and sees, hears, walks, stands, eats, and drinks; with the angels, that he has knowledge and understanding.

He is *nothing,* since whatever he is, he is such by the appointment of God. What is the shadow compared to the body? Nothing. Whatsoever man *hath* is not his own, but God's. The jewels do not belong to the casket, but to him who places them therein, and has power to remove them thence whenever he will. Has man beauty? It is not his, but God's. How soon may a beautiful color fade, a beautiful skin become wrinkled! Has he wisdom? It is God's: for it is easy to God to deprive a boasting Nebuchadnezzar of his intellect, and reduce him to the level of the cattle of the field. Whatever good a man *does* is not his, but God's. He is only the instrument employed in the hand of God. "Not I, but the grace of God that was with me," 1 Cor. 15:10.

All, and yet nothing, is *the description of the true Christian.*

He is *all,* since he is daily conformed more and more to the image of Him who is "all in all," and in whom he findeth "all things." He is all, since he becomes all things to all men, that he may gain some, 1 Cor. 9:22.

He is *nothing,* since he possesses nothing of himself, since he arrogates nothing to himself, and in all things gives God the glory.

I recollect that I once described a true Christian thus: "He is one who at all times is poor in spirit, for he has in his natural and sinful state nothing; therefore he deems himself little, yea, he despises himself, and is willing to be despised by others; thinks nothing of all his works, and desires not to be esteemed for them; sees God in Christ as his God and Savior, and the source of all the good that is wrought in him, or which he is enabled to do;

therefore he thinketh of himself as nothing, but gives God alone the glory." And thus I think still. Examine yourself by this test.

ON

THE DESIRE OF LIFE

I FIND one thing which I have; I seek one thing which I have not. The former makes life bitter; the latter makes death sweet. I find that "in me, that is, in my flesh, dwelleth no good thing. O wretched man that I am! who shall deliver me from the body of this death?" Rom. 7:18, 24. I seek Him whom my soul loveth. I desire to depart, and be with Christ. Where would I rather he than with my Savior? Where doth the bride prefer to be rather than with the bridegroom? Come, Lord Jesus, come quickly.

But have you a desire to live? Hearken and I will tell you what life is. When a certain wise man was asked what he did? he answered, "I am gradually dying." And he spoke justly. For our life begins to decline as soon as it begins to advance. How unwise not to have a desire to die, and yet you die daily! You would only die slowly, but so much the greater is the pain. You wish to live, and yet continue so long in the act of dying. You seek not that true life which is attained through a happy death. Hear yet farther what is life: it is much evil to endure, much evil to see, or much evil to perpetrate. The endurance of evil is painful, and pain freezes the heart. The sight of evil gives rise to disquietude and distress, and these rend the heart. The commission of evil causes an accusing and tormenting conscience; and this is a hell. If you have a desire of life, live so that you may live evermore. Hear lastly what St. Bernard says; "The bad the worse, and the worst has the world! The good the better, and the best has heaven." I choose the best. Do thou likewise.

ON

A RIGHTLY DIRECTED LOVE

THERE are four objects especially to which our love has respect—to sin, to ourselves, to our neighbor, and to God.

Sin we must not at all love. Whosoever loves sin, hates God, himself, and his neighbor. He displeases God, he destroys himself, he injures his neighbor. *Ourselves* and *our neighbor* we may love; but not too much: ourselves in subordination to God, not above him. I love myself, and therefore am thankful that I live in the enjoyment of health: should it please God to visit me with sickness, His will be done! *Our neighbor* we should love in God, not out of God. When I love my neighbor, I regard him with sincere friendship; if he should transgress, I reprove him for his fault. It is *God* only that I cannot love too much. I cannot thank him too much for his benefits, which I do not deserve. Who can give him anything in return? He hath created and redeemed thee; what canst thou render unto him again? He can receive love from thee in return, and nothing else; and yet love has first come from Him. How can you love Him too much, who hath loved you with an everlasting love? If you give your chief love to the world, it makes you no return of love. It shall be my endeavor and earnest prayer henceforward to love God supremely; myself and all things in Him; yea, even to hate myself and all things for his sake. Let this be your care also.

ON BENEVOLENCE

WE should "remember the words of the Lord Jesus, how he said, It is more blessed to give than to receive," Acts 20:35. The world thinks not so. It chooses rather to receive than give. "By giving much," it says, "a man becomes poor." I say, To give is more blessed than to receive; and it is good to dispense liberally. Two husbandmen sow their seed in different parts of the same field; one abundantly, the other with too sparing a hand. Whether of the two shall receive the largest increase? And is it not so in spiritual things? "He which soweth sparingly shall reap also sparingly; and he which soweth bountifully shall reap also bountifully," 2 Cor. 9:5. The seed is not lost which is cast into the ground. It springs forth, and bears fruit with much increase. Giving in faith, and from Christian motives, makes no man poor, but many rich. He that thus giveth, lendeth unto the Lord, and look, that which he layeth out shall be paid him again, Prov. 19:17. Give, and it shall be given unto you. The more you are like unto God, the happier you shall be; and God receives not, but gives. God is good; thence his name; and it is the character of goodness to delight in communicating blessings. Why should I not give a few crumbs to my Savior, who daily supplieth my table, and giveth me all things richly to enjoy? Do you wish to receive more from him? Then give the more. Whilst you dispense, you receive from him; whilst blessing others, you are blessed yourself.

ON

THE CONFLICT BETWEEN THE FLESH AND SPIRIT

EVIL spirits, as well as angels, surround the Christian. The former cast a stone in his way, that he may stumble and fall; the latter bear him up in their arms, that he may not dash his foot against the stone. They contend for him, as Michael and the devil contended for the body of Moses. If there were no conflict, there would be no victory. And I know that the victory must be on God's side. As much as Satan would alarm me, so much doth the angel of God comfort me; and I bless God for his mercy.

Nor is the conflict carried on only without, but also within the child of God. "The flesh lusteth against the Spirit, and the Spirit against the flesh: and these are contrary the one to the other," Gal. 5:17. The flesh betrays man through its "deceitful lusts," Eph. 4:22, as the fish is ensnared by the deceptive bait. It sets forth the advantages which we may expect from sin; though never has any one sought them by such unlawful means, without losing much more than he gains. "For what is a man profited, if he shall gain the whole world, and lose his own soul? or what shall a man give in exchange for his soul?" Matt 16:26. If you attain that which is really good, then serve God; for "godliness is profitable unto all things, having promise of the life that now is, and of that which is to come," 1 Tim. 4:8.

The flesh sometimes entices us by the pleasures and joys which are the fruit of sin; but how vain are its promises! "Though wickedness be sweet in his mouth," says Zophar, the Naamathite, "though he hide it under his tongue; though he spare it, and forsake it not; but keep it still within his mouth: yet his meat in his bowels is turned, it is the gall of asps within him," Job 20:12–14. Wickedness is like a sweet morsel, which a man taketh into his mouth, but when swallowed, it becomes bitter as gall and wormwood. Would you possess real joys, why do you not seek them in the Lord? "For the kingdom of God is not meat and drink; but righteousness, and peace, and joy in the Holy Ghost," Rom. 14:17.

Honor and renown are also promised by the flesh; but here, too, doth it act the part of a deceiver. It is poor honor which arises from sin. Honor is the accompaniment of virtue; shame and sorrow of sin. "What fruit," says the apostle, "had ye then in those things whereof ye are now ashamed? for the end of those things is death," Rom. 6:21. Would you possess honor, be the servant of the Lord. "If any man serve me," saith he, "let him follow me; and where I am, there shall also my servant be: if any man serve me, him will my Father honor," John 12:26.

Sometimes the flesh promises the favor and friendship of the great. But can friendship be without love, and love without God? How can God and sin exist together? Piety is the true means of acquiring real friendship; for "when a man's ways please the Lord, he maketh even his enemies to be at peace with him," Prov. 16:7.

And who can number all the seductions of the flesh? It is a murderer, as was the devil from the beginning, for "if ye live after the flesh, ye shall die." But, on the other hand, "if ye through the Spirit do mortify the deeds of the body, ye shall live," Rom. 8:13. And this conflict is ever carried on within us; "for the flesh lusteth against the Spirit, and the Spirit against the flesh: and these are contrary the one to the other: so that ye cannot do the things that ye would," Gal. 5:17. To how many evil thoughts does the flesh give rise? They are as wicked angels, that would hurry you with them to hell. How many good thoughts doth the Spirit infuse? They are as holy angels, who would convey you to heaven. How much better are angels than devils! Choose for yourself a guide. Should you follow the wicked one, I will nevertheless follow the messenger of heaven. Should you hasten to the pit of destruction, I will ascend to the dwelling-place of God—and tell me, who has chosen the better portion?

ON

THE POWER OF FAITH

"THY faith hath saved thee," Luke 7:50. This is indeed an assurance full of the sweetest comfort. I would not exchange it for all the treasures of the world. "Thy faith hath saved thee"—but what? Is it not Jesus who saves? It is, hut he puts honor on faith; as when a rich man places a piece of gold in the hand of a beggar, and says to him, "See, thy hand has made thee rich." God attributes not his benefits to his own goodness, but to our faith, that we may know when we receive not something which we greatly desire, and stand in much need of, that it is from want not of his mercy, but of our faith. Whosoever does not believe, is wavering and uncertain whether God will bestow the blessing or not. Such a man receives not the things that he asks. If he ask of God "that giveth to all men liberally, and upbraideth not, it shall be given him. But let him ask in faith, nothing wavering. For he that wavereth is like a wave of the sea driven with the wind and tossed. For let not that man think that he shall receive any thing of the Lord," James 1:5–7. God will give him nothing. It is just as when a man holds a vessel in his hand, and does not keep it still, nothing can be poured into it. God will not pour out his goodness in vain, that it may not be abused. As you believe, so shall it be done unto you. The word of God must not remain without effect; it becomes operative when apprehended by faith. God has promised you support in time of famine; believe, and you shall receive it; bread shall be provided for you, even the stones, if needful, shall become bread. If you succeed not as well as you could wish, your unbelief is the cause. In faith is wealth, in unbelief is poverty; in faith is heaven, in unbelief is hell; in faith is all things, in unbelief is nothing. If it go ill with me, I have myself only to blame and my unbelief; if it go well with me, I give thanks to the God of all goodness and grace, for He it is that both worketh faith in me, and crowneth it with success.

ON GRATITUDE

IT is related of one of the ten lepers whom our Lord cleansed, that "when he saw that he was healed, he turned back, and with a loud voice glorified God, and fell down on his face at his feet, giving him thanks: and he was a Samaritan," Luke 17:15, 16. "Turning back" is therefore the best thanksgiving.

You give God praise *with your mouth;* you do well. He delighteth in such offerings, and the more you open your mouth wide, the more he will fill it. Every thanksgiving draws down a fresh benefit. The rivers arise out of the sea, and return to their source. Prayer brings the stream of Divine grace from on high; thanksgiving conducts it back again. The goodness of God is like Jacob's ladder, on which the angels of God are continually ascending and descending. The prayer of faith ascends to God; the blessing of grace descends to men. The grateful heart ascends, and a rich communication of heavenly love descends to refresh and strengthen it yet more. All things tend towards their source, that they may rest; and thus also do the blessings conferred by the God of heaven.

But tell me, do you praise God *with your life?* Turning back is the best expression of gratitude. Consider your ways. Where are you? Your Savior exhorts you, "Enter ye in at the strait gate: for wide is the gate, and broad is the way, that leadeth to destruction, and many there be which go in thereat," Matt 7:13. Are you on that way? Do you travel with the multitude? Do you live like the world? "Because strait is the gate, and narrow is the way which leadeth unto life, and few there be that find it," verse 14. Are you among the few? Whither is your path conducting you? Look well to your footsteps. Pride, wrath, hatred, malice, pomp, avarice, unmercifullness, falsehood—these are the footsteps of the world. Humility, gentleness, love, righteousness, contentment, mercy, truth—these are the footsteps of Jesus. Where are you? Turn back; O turn back if you are not in the right way. By conversion man giveth praise to God. "Let your light so shine before men, that they may see your good works, and glorify your Father which is in heaven," Matt. 5:16.

I ask once more, Do you praise God *in suffering?* Patience is a lovely thank-offering. God gives you this world's goods. You say, "The Lord hath given, his name be praised:" but God takes them from you, do you not also say, "The Lord hath taken away, blessed be the name of the Lord?" A patient heart is always prepared to "turn back" to God. Whatever God bestows, it readily yields back, if it should please God. I will give thanks to God with my lips, my heart, my life, and in all my sufferings. All that is within me shall praise the Lord.

ON INGRATITUDE

NOTHING is more common in the world than ingratitude, and especially towards God. You are displeased when you read the account of the lepers who were cleansed, that only one of the ten returned to give thanks unto God. But why are you displeased with others, and not rather with yourself? Look into your own bosom, you will find an ungrateful guest therein. How often have you given God thanks for your health, which is yet more precious than gold? How often have you thanked him that he has cleansed you from the leprosy of sin? I frequently wonder how it comes to pass that out of a hundred who request the prayers of the congregation, scarcely ten are found to return thanks. Is aid, then, rendered to so few? No; hut ingratitude is not sensible of the aid. How much gratitude do you express to your friend who gives you a present, or an allowance out of his abundance! but how different is your conduct towards God, who has given you all that you possess! One only in ten turns back to give God thanks. My friend, avoid that shameful sin of ingratitude. An ungrateful man is guilty of many sins, and sensible of no kindness. He is hateful to God and men. He stops the stream of goodness, which otherwise would flow onwards in its gentle course. It is the part of a Christian soon to forget injuries, but never benefits. How many blessings does God confer upon the world! But who gives him thanks? At how great a price did Jesus redeem men! But who thinks of it? Who thanks him for it? Do not expect for yourself a better lot than that of Jesus. As you do not undertake anything for the sake of thanks, so should you also not refrain from doing good because men are ungrateful. Love is not weary in well-doing. It is a good tree which yields much fruit, and does not withhold it from him who shakes and agitates it.

I will shun ingratitude as the most base and disgraceful vice, and the parent of innumerable sins; and will be content, even though men should render me evil for good.

ON

THE EVIDENCE OF FAITH

To promise much, and to perform little, is common both to old and young. You say, "I am a Christian; I believe in God the Father, in Jesus Christ the Redeemer, and in the Holy Ghost, the Sanctifier of all the elect people of God, and I love my neighbor." The words I hear, but where are the proofs? It was a saying of Cicero, who was a pagan, "It would be ill for me if my words justified me more than my deeds." My friend, is it not an evil case when your words speak in your favor, and not your works? Let your daily walk commend you, and I will believe your profession. Better are silent lips and an eloquent hand, than eloquent lips and a silent hand. If a negro were to declare to you that he was white, and you saw with your eyes that he was black, would you believe him? You say that God is your Father, but I perceive not that you walk before him in filial love, fear, confidence, and obedience. Am I then wrong in not relying on your words? You say, "I believe that Jesus hath redeemed me from sin and death." These words are good, but what do I behold? You serve sin, and precipitate yourself into death. How do these things accord: to be delivered from sin, and yet to serve sin; to be freed from death, and yet to yield yourself up to its power! You say, "I love my neighbor." That is indeed well if it be true; but how am I permitted to see that neither his bodily nor spiritual necessities affect your heart?

He mourns, and you speak not to him one word of comfort. He goes astray, and you bring him not back; he transgresses before your eyes, and yet you chide him not; he is hungry, thirsty, and naked, and yet you do not feed him, nor give him drink, nor clothe him; he is sick, and you do not visit him. Rather tell me candidly what I see, than profess it is otherwise. Show me the faith which you say you possess; let your love be made manifest in works of righteousness. Are you not aware that men know the tree by its fruit, and prove the profession by the practice? My eyes and ears must be satisfied, or I will not give credit to what you profess. "Go and show yourselves to the priest," was the command of Christ. Show yourself by your works, or I trust you not. Chrysostom says, "God will not be honored with words only, since it is not thus that he honors us; but with deeds and substantial realities." When we give him praise, not only with our lips, but with our lives, it is then that we show him honor. I will, through grace, do what I profess, and corroborate my words by my works. It was the description of Jesus that he was "mighty in word and deed," Luke 24:19. Our deeds should verify our words, and they will give to them power and energy. By the help of my God it shall be so with me.

ON THE

LAST WILL AND TESTAMENT OF A CHRISTIAN

"SET thine house in order: for thou shalt die, and not live," Isaiah 38:1. Thank God, I am ready! my last will and testament is prepared.

My Father, who art in heaven, and who hast created me, I yield up my spirit to thee. Thou hast given it to me, I return it to thee again. In thy hands it is in safe keeping. I adopt the words of my Savior himself, "Father, into thy hands I commend my spirit," Luke 23:46.

My Savior, who hast redeemed me, I leave my sins with thee. O blot them out, thou Lamb of God, that takest away the sins of the world. Cast them into the fountain of thy blood, that they may be remembered against me no more forever.

O *Holy Ghost,* the Comforter, who hast so often refreshed me with heavenly consolations, to thee I direct my last look as my life is fading away. When I can no longer speak, then make intercession for me before God, with groanings that cannot be uttered; when I can no more hear, whisper comfort to my soul; when I can no more see, enlighten mine eyes, that I sleep not the sleep of death.

Ye *angels of God,* who have borne me up in your hands, yours shall be my tears which I daily shed over my sins, and which have been precious in your sight. I know "that there is joy in the presence of the angels of God over one sinner that repenteth," Luke 15:10.

Satan, wouldst thou have something? All the good works which were not the fruit of faith I leave to thee. Take them hence.

O *earth,* thou art my mother; and hast for so many years, by the power of God, administered to my support, I will therefore commit my body to thee. "Naked came I out of my mother's womb, and naked shall I return to it again," Job 1:21. I desire no splendid rites of sepulture.

My beloved wife, I entrust you to Him who is called the Defender of the widow. Should you find no justice upon earth, remain only faithful to him, and he will defend your cause. In want he will care for you; in oppression he will deliver you; in sorrow he will comfort you. Commit all your griefs and cares to him. I will not counsel the world not to harass you, for afflictions are salutary, and God ruleth over all. "He will not despise the supplication of the widow, when she poureth out her complaint. Do not the tears run down the widow's cheeks? and is not her cry against him that causeth them to fall?" Ecclesiasticus 35:14, 15.

Dear children, I choose for you a better Father than you had in me; even Him "of whom the whole family in heaven and earth is named," Eph. 3:15. He who is the Father of the fatherless will therefore be your Father. He who careth for the young ravens will not remit his care for you. Take heed that you serve him, and walk in his ways. He will be the Guide of your youth, and your portion forever.

My friends, I leave you to a gracious God, who is the best of friends.

You, *my little flock,* shall be remembered by me in heaven. Though you may forget me and mine, I will never be unmindful of you.

For *the poor,* I have the blessing of a rich God, the possessor of heaven and earth, which I ask for you in faith. More I have not. Silver and gold have I none; and it were a shame if I had. Whatever a servant of God can spare belongs to the poor.

This is my last will, and I will cheerfully close my eyes in the arms of Jesus whenever it shall please God to call me hence.

ON

LOVE TO ONE'S SELF

YOU are the best friend to yourself. I will explain to you what I mean. St. Paul says "Love worketh no ill to his neighbor," Rom. 13:10. Whoever inflicts an injury on another, loves him not; and the more severe the infliction, the less the love. Now, tell me, who does the greatest harm to you? Is it Satan? Can he hurt you? No; he has not the least power over you. He can but tempt you to wrong. Is it death? He is deprived of his sting. Is it the world? What can it take from you when you have nothing that is your own? It is yourself that is your greatest enemy. You would be rich, and yet you will not lay up satisfying and abiding treasures in heaven; you would be great, and yet you do not subdue your passions, and you despise the glory that is in Christ; you would possess joy, and yet you make to yourself sorrow, and freeze up your heart without cause; you would live long, and yet you destroy yourself by sin, and cut off the remnant of your days; you would be happy, and yet by thoughtlessness and carnal security lose your inheritance. How, then, can you say that you are not your worst enemy?

But who is it that loves you? God, and your faithful friend. God loves you, and seeks to make you happy. He chastens you, that you may not perish with the world; he gives you not what you wish, but that which is for your soul's health. What father puts into the hand of his child a sharp knife or razor? What physician gives his patient that which may he pleasant to the taste, but injurious, or, at least, of no service. God loves you, and therefore he is as a physician and father, not as an enemy and destroyer. Your friend sees you transgress, and reproves you; he loves you, and would rescue you from destruction. Acknowledge this, and be grateful. Do you now inquire who is your neighbor? Tell me who was neighbor to the man that fell among thieves, and was left in the way almost dead? Was it not he who had compassion on him? And who has the most compassion on you? Certainly not yourself.

ON

GIVING TO THE POOR

IT is good to lend unto the Lord. What I lend unto Him, he restores to me in a better state. I give him a heart that is unholy and polluted, and receive from him one that is renewed and made clean. He gives to me more than he receives. I sow a few grains of corn, and am enriched by him with a plentiful harvest. The widow of Zarephath gave to the prophet a little cake, and her barrel of meal did not waste, neither did her cruise of oil fail. To render unto God the things that are God's, is the ready way to an abundant increase. For if you give, it shall be given unto you again, full measure, pressed down, and running over.

"Thine" and "mine" follow each other closely in the Lord's prayer. Thy name, thy kingdom, thy will, precede; my daily bread, follows. When the precept "give" is obeyed with alacrity, and with a liberal hand, the promise, "It shall be given unto you again," Luke 6:38, is yet more richly fulfilled. Giving alms maketh not poor. When you comfort the heart of the poor with a piece of bread, or a cup of cold water, it is not forgotten of God. The believing poor repay you with a prayer. The prayer of faith is heard in heaven, and followed by a blessing.

As thou believest, so shall it be done unto thee. Whatsoever a man doeth in unbelief is all lost; that, on the other hand, which is done in faith, is gain. Such as is the seed, such is also the harvest; with the merciful God will show himself merciful, 2 Sam. 22:26. I will gladly share my substance with my God. For one-half he giveth a full measure. He *can* do it, because he is richer than I; he *will* do it, for he is goodness itself. For this I have the hand and seal of God, and on these I confidently rely. Are they not His own words, "He which soweth bountifully shall reap also bountifully?" 2 Cor. 9:6. I will therefore scatter the seed with a full hand. The Holy Spirit seals the assurance in my heart that, through grace, the harvest shall be great. The hand and seal of God cannot deceive. If you see not today the harvest, yet it will come to-morrow; or if not before, yet certainly in the day of judgment. If through faith, and for the glory of God, I make to myself friends of the mammon of unrighteousness, they will hereafter receive me into everlasting habitations, and I shall yet hear those gracious words of my Savior, and my God and Savior, "Come, ye blessed of my Father, inherit the kingdom prepared for you from the foundation of the world: for I was an hungered, and ye gave me meat: I was thirsty, and ye gave me drink: I was a stranger, and ye took me in: naked, and ye clothed me: I was sick, and ye visited me," Matt. 25:34–36. Is it not, then, good to lend unto the Lord? Blessed are they that see not, and yet believe, John 20:29.

ON

THE RICHES OF A CHRISTIAN

I POSSESS all things. What lack I then? I have never met with a richer man in the world, than he who can adopt the language of the 73rd Psalm, "Whom have I in heaven but thee? and there is none upon earth that I desire beside thee. My flesh and my heart faileth: but God is the strength of my heart, and my portion forever," ver. 25, 26. Whosoever can utter in faith the two words, "my God," is rich beyond all others. Whoever cannot say these words, hath nothing; for we are only stewards, God is our master. All things are His. He alone is ours; out of Him we have nothing. Is God not mine, then nothing is mine; for in him I find all things: and what belongs to the father belongs also to the son, as to one who hath nothing, and yet possesseth all things, 2 Cor. 6:10.

The world affords me no pleasures, presents me with no gifts; in God alone have I unfailing enjoyment. The men of the world seek their many things from many sources, and for their supposed benefits they are beholden to many. I seek my all in One; my obligations are therefore centered in One only. To desire nothing more is the best riches; yet this is as rare as it is excellent. Never enough, always more, is the language of most men; and the more they have, the more they want. Nothing more, already enough, is said by few. Our desires are never satisfied but in God; there they find an inexhaustible fullness. Not to find enough in God is the mark either of insatiable avarice, or of a mean and grovelling spirit. However rich I am today, I may be poor to-morrow. Happy is he who can say from the heart, "Thou art my God, my joy, my life. Whatsoever thou art, that art thou to me. Whatsoever thou hast, all is mine. Whatsoever thou doest, is approved of me as the best. Thou art my Father, even when thou correctest me with the rod; and I am thy beloved child, and thou wilt never forsake me." How rich and happy is such a one in God! But the sense of this blessed relationship is sometimes lost amid the sobs and tears of correction. May I never doubt his fatherly love. I know my God, and am persuaded of his good will towards me. The most weak and feeble children are the most tenderly beloved. Being one of the little ones of God, and but as an infant before him, he carries me in his bosom. The cry of the feeble entereth into his ears. If I cannot cry, I will yet look upwards; if I cannot say "Father," yet "Abba" will be enough. It is my desire to be always able to say "My God;" and that desire hath He himself wrought in me. How can he despise the work of his own hands? I shall not refrain from saying in my greatest weakness, "O that I could believe that God were my God!" "Blessed are they which do hunger and thirst after righteousness: for they shall be filled," Matt. 5:6. Whosoever desires to have, possesses already that which he desires, or may at least assure himself that he shall yet have it.

A humble poverty is often better than a haughty superfluity. Many a one is poor amidst great possessions, and many a one is rich in the greatest want. I will not hasten to be rich. Perhaps I am more pleasing to God in my penury, than others in their fullness of bread. How can I be satisfied with that which I have, if I am longing to receive that which I have not? Doth it please God to scatter riches into the lap of others from a full horn, but to impart to me only a slender supply, shall I therefore repine? Even in one drop of cold water he giveth me more than I deserve, more than I can repay him in the whole of my life. I will thankfully receive the earnest as a pledge of a full harvest; and who knows whether he may not yet give me more manna in my vessel, and more oil in my cruise? How many crumbs fall from the rich man's table, which a poor Lazarus would fain receive, if they were given to him! He who is weak in health, eats often, and takes but little at a time. It may be, that I cannot in my weakness make use of more than that which my God giveth me.

ON

THE SOCIETY OF A CHRISTIAN

ALONE, and yet not alone. I wish to be alone, for I have no desire to associate with a false world, which loves and commends only that which, with itself, lieth in wickedness; which hates, calumniates, and persecutes the good. Yet am I never alone; and therefore I have not that to fear, of which the wise man speaks, "Woe to him that is alone when he falleth; for he hath not another to help him up," Eccles. 4:10. My God is at all times, and in all places, with me. Do I stumble? he supports me. Do I fall? he lifts me up. My friend visits me, but remains not with me; as he comes, so doth he go away again. I have no need to ask God to come to me; he dwelleth already in me, and is as near to me as myself; nor need I be careful lest he should depart. He never leaveth nor forsaketh the child whom he loves. Of this I am well assured. He may hide himself from me, but will never utterly depart.

If I have some of my fellow creatures with me, can I the more confide in a false and faithless world? And even if they are my best friends, how can I divest myself of the care, lest I should offend them, or they me? Should they fall, it may not be in my power to lift them up; or should I fall, they likewise may be incapable of rendering me assistance. Or, it may be, that we fall, both I and my friends, together. I will not be anxious about society. Men may pull down more in one hour, than I can build up in a whole year. If I have but God with me in the depth of my heart, He is better to me than a thousand friends. Should the powers of earth and hell wage war against me, with the help of my God, they shall be put to flight. Happy is he that is ever, and yet never, alone.

ON THE

SUFFERINGS OF A CHRISTIAN

"It is not right," you say, when any injury is inflicted on you; "they do me injustice." I say, "It is neither right nor wrong." That the world treats you ill, is not right; that you suffer, is not wrong, for to that are you called. To do good, and to suffer for it, is the part of a Christian. Tell me, Was it not right that Jesus suffered? Yes, for such was the will of God, and thus did he atone for sin. Nor is it otherwise than right that you suffer, for God has appointed you thereto, and you have richly merited it by your sins. How can you speak of right, when that which you receive is so far from your due! Had you been dealt with in strict justice, you would long ago have been cast, both body and soul, into hell. But God dealeth with you in grace, and not according to your deserts. If you had your due, Satan might claim you as his own, but grace makes you the servant of God. When, therefore, afflictions arise, say to your soul, "Be content to bear them, the will of the Lord be done." It is of grace that God lays aside the scourge, and corrects you with a Father's love.

I will never complain of wrong, for my trials come from God, who deals not with me in justice, nor yet unjustly. All that he doeth is only grace. Does the world come too near to me? It has no right to do so, for I belong not to the world, but to God. Yet I will not quarrel with the stone, but observe the hand by which it is cast. God will answer for me; to him I commit my cause. "I will bear the indignation of the Lord, because I have sinned against him, until he plead my cause, and execute judgment for me: he will bring me forth to the light, and I shall behold his righteousness," Micah 7:9.

ON

THE REST OF THE SOUL

REST is the chief of blessings. Where doth God rest? In your heart? Children are wont to rest on the bosom of their mother, but here the Father rests on that of his child. After the creation of man, God rested, because his rest was to be in man. He seeks to dwell in your heart.

And where can your soul find rest? In God, and nowhere else. Place a sick child where you will, it is never easier than in its mother's lap. "The soul," saith Augustine, "is made for eternity, and can therefore find no rest till it finds it in the eternal God." Tell me, when is your state best? When you are rich? No; with much wealth there is much care. No man can sleep sweetly upon thorns. When you are held in high estimation and honor? No; as surely as the shadow follows the body, so certainly are earthly elevations accompanied by envy, hatred, and disquiet. When you sleep on a downy bed? Oh, no; how many fearful dreams, how many nightly terrors may then surround you! I know of no greater happiness than to have a God of grace as my God. For where desire ends, there enjoyment begins. Now, there is nothing in heaven or in earth which can satisfy desire, but the grace of God. In that alone can I find unalloyed pleasure. In Jesus I find the grace of God; in Jesus I find rest. How tenderly and lovingly doth he invite and allure me, "Come unto me, all ye that labor and are heavy laden, and I will give you rest. Take my yoke upon you, and learn of me; for I am meek and lowly in heart: and ye shall find rest unto your souls," Matt. 11:28, 29. Yes, my Savior, I give thee my heart as thine own, and will seek my rest only in thee. Whether I live, I will live unto the Lord; and whether I die, I will die unto the Lord: thus in life shall I have peace, and in death joy, living and dying I shall be his. Amen.

ON

TAMING THE TONGUE

THE tongue is in a slippery place; it is no wonder that man in his speech often stumbles and falls. In such a place there is no security, unless men walk with caution, and watch every footstep. "The tongue is a little member, and boasteth great things. Behold, how great a matter a little fire kindleth! And the tongue is a fire, a world of iniquity: so is the tongue among our members, that it defileth the whole body, and setteth on fire the course of nature; and it is set on fire of hell. For every kind of beasts, and of birds, and of serpents, and of things in the sea, is tamed, and hath been tamed of mankind: but the tongue can no man tame; it is an unruly evil, full of deadly poison," James 3:5–8. For as the serpent conceals its poison beneath the tongue, so does the tongue cover a poison, fatal to both body and soul. It is like a wild vicious horse. Give loose to the reins, and it will carry you into a thousand by-ways, and defy all control. Curb it with the bridle of a wise and considerate discipline. "Behold, we put bits in the horses' mouths, that they may obey us; and we turn about their whole body. Behold also the ships, which though they be so great, and are driven of fierce winds, yet are they turned about with a very small helm, whithersoever the governor listeth," James 3:3, 4. How wisely does David speak, "I will take heed to my ways, that I sin not with my tongue: I will keep my mouth with a bridle, while the wicked is before me," Psa. 39:1. Thus take heed to your ways; set the Lord before your face, that you may not offend with the tongue. Nature has connected the tongue by one ligament with the heart, by another with the brain. Consider this, and act wisely. Before all things, seek that your heart may be made pure.

As no sweetness is found in the sea, so no wholesome discourse proceeds from a corrupt and impure heart. "Out of the abundance of the heart the mouth speaketh. A good man out of the good treasure of the heart bringeth forth good things: and an evil man out of the evil treasure bringeth forth evil things," Matt. 12:34, 35. Your heart cannot, indeed, in this fallen state, be so perfectly cleansed from every root of evil and bitterness as to have none remaining. And, therefore, even the most holy men are in danger of offending with the tongue. Moses himself spake unadvisedly with his lips. See, therefore, that you exercise a godly jealousy over yourself, and take heed lest the mouth and the heart be divided and opposed. What God has united, you must not separate. Words bear witness of the heart, let them not give a false testimony. That which the mouth speaks, the heart should experience, and that which the heart intends, the mouth should declare.

Beware, then, of being hasty and thoughtless in your words, uttering only what falls from the tongue. Take counsel with the head, and well consider what you would say before you give it expression. It is good advice which St. James gives us, "Be slow to speak," James 1:19. A Christian should not allow one word to escape his lips, before he has first considered whether he might thereby dishonor God, injure or distress his neighbor, or trouble his own conscience. O that I might place bars upon my mouth, and a seal upon my lips, that I might not transgress with my tongue! I look for the help of my God.

ON

AN UNDIVIDED HEART

THE heart should not be divided. I say to the hypocrite, God has given you *two eyes*, that you may look both above and beneath you; that you may contemplate both heaven and hell. He has given you *two ears*, that you may hearken both to the accuser and the accused, when you have to judge between them; *two hands*, that you may raise one upwards to God, and receive, and stretch forth the other towards your neighbor, and give; *two feet*, that you may serve yourself and your master; but you have only *one head*, and *one heart*. God approves not of those who are double-minded, or double-tongued; from whose lips comes forth at the same time that which is cold and hot; and who speak not the same when they sit as when they stand; who divide their heart between Him and the devil.

A double-hearted man is a monster, which God will not accept as an offering. God demands an undivided heart. Such, also, is the demand of Satan; for though he may not immediately persuade you that you should give him your heart, and seems to be satisfied with a part of it, yet he aims at the whole. He knows full well that God will not receive a divided heart, and that therefore the whole shall yet be his own, being rejected of God.

The heart is but of small capacity; but if it were greater, it would be your duty to make it the undivided dwelling-place of Him from whom you have received it, and who alone can make it better. Who has given you authority to dispose of that which was not yours, but God's? To Him the whole belongs, and not merely a portion. How is it possible that you can unite God and Satan within you? How can they both take a part of *one heart?* Satan tempts to that which is evil; God moves you to that which is good. God destroys the work of Satan; Satan, on the other hand, would throw down the work of God. Where God dwells is heaven, where Satan dwells is hell. How can your heart, at the same time, be in heaven and in hell? Where God dwells, he is served and obeyed; where Satan dwells, he also is obeyed. Can you serve two masters so opposite in every respect?

God has given me my whole heart, not to use it at its uncontrolled possessor, but as a steward, answerable to Him. I will, by his grace, not abuse my trust; but restore him his own. My heart is His, not mine!

ON CALUMNY

THREE swords on one tongue; are they not too many? I refer to the calumniator. He wounds three at once—himself, the person calumniated, and the silent listener to his calumny. Lying and murder are not divided. Our Lord said of Satan that he was a liar and murderer from the beginning, John 8:44. The calumniator is no better; he is possessed of the nature of the devil, and is his tool. As no man is secure from the assaults of Satan, neither is he exempt from the voice of detraction; and as no man can control the enemy of souls, so can he not tame a wicked tongue. Let him think of this who invents audacious lies against his neighbor: he hath a devil. Satan obtained admission into paradise in the form of the serpent, who carried poison under his tongue. With a false tongue did he pierce and instill his poison.

No sword cuts more sharply, no barb penetrates more deeply, no wound causes more exquisite pain, than calumny. "The stroke of the whip maketh marks in the flesh: but the stroke of the tongue breaketh the bones. Many have fallen by the edge of the sword: but not so many as have fallen by the tongue," Ecclesiasticus 28:17, 18.

There are no wounds so difficult to heal as those made by the slanderer. Yet I will not be cast down, if I be assaulted by the tongue of the wicked. When I cry unto God in my prayer, the head of the serpent is wounded; and I know well that he will not depart, without attempting to hurt me by the tongue of falsehood. But he cannot in reality inflict an injury. Let the calumniator say what he will, he must give an account thereof in the day of judgment. "With me it is a very small thing that I should be judged of you, or of man's judgment," 1 Cor. 4:3. My commendation consisteth not in the opinion of men, but in the approval of God, and the testimony of my conscience. If I am not better for the praise of man, neither am I worse for his detraction. I am known to God. It is well with him who hath praise of God. Meanwhile, my works, wrought by his grace, shall justify me, and stop the mouth of slander. Calumny lives not long; truth loves the light, and I will wait for the God of truth, and "he shall bring forth my righteousness as the light, and my judgment as the noonday," Psalm 37:6.

ON THE

BROAD AND NARROW WAY

KEEP company with the few—with the one, and not with the nine. This is good counsel, do not reject it. Hear what our Lord saith, "Enter ye in at the strait gate: for wide is the gate, and broad is the way, that leadeth to destruction, and many there be which go in thereat: because strait is the gate, and narrow is the way, which leadeth unto life, and few there be that find it," Matt. 7:13, 14. You say, "As liveth the multitude so will I live. Who can swim alone against the stream?" My friend, the multitude are on their way to destruction, will you go with them? I counsel you not. The fire of hell rageth fiercely; the worm dieth not. Few hit the mark, many shoot near it. Few receive the prize, while many run in vain. Few gain the crown, and attain salvation: let your lot be with the few, and you shall be saved. The children of the world are not true guides; they are not safe lights, but deceptive meteors. Be not like the world. If it be difficult to swim against the stream, remember that it is always easier to do evil than good. Your nature is inclined to that which is evil, and has abundant means of gratifying its propensities: it is opposed to that which is good, and has many hinderances.

Are you derided by the multitude? forget not that you are a stranger and foreigner, who may expect to suffer wrong; to whom the children of the wicked one point the finger in mockery. How was it with the apostles, the chosen of God? Hear what St. Paul saith, "God hath set forth us the apostles last, as it were appointed to death, for we are made a spectacle unto the world: and to angels, and to men. We are made as the filth of the earth, and are the offscouring of all things unto this day," 1 Cor. 4:9, 13. Say with David, "I will yet be more vile than thus" before the Lord, 2 Sam. 6:22. I will cheerfully cast in my lot with the few and the least, for the many and the great are with the wicked. I will not, in any of my works, regard the example of the multitude, but I will look to the will of my God, who will teach me to distinguish good from evil. If that which I do, please not the multitude, I will not repine. I seek to be approved in God's sight, and to give him honor as my Father; and also in the sight of the people of God, and to contribute to their edification.

ON THE

LOVE OF HEAVENLY THINGS

I AM not where I appear to be. I live upon the earth, but my life is in heaven; for my affections are set upon things above, not upon things on the earth. Even whilst united to this tabernacle of the body, the soul is in heaven, as imprisoned, and yet free. We say of a wrathful man, He has lost himself; and we say it correctly: and so it is with all the children of this world; they lose their souls whilst they love earthly things. Their soul is laden with thick clay; the jewel is buried in the mire. Through grace I am enabled to look upwards. Heaven is better than the earth, for God hath prepared it for his friends. Is not the Creator above the creatures? Are not the friends of God more honored by him than his enemies?

The eyes, saith one, are the guides of love. Do we not see more of the heavens than of the earth? Mine eye can only look at a few miles of the earth, but it taketh in the whole compass of the heavens. God hath placed the earth under my feet; the heavens he hath spread abroad over my head. And why? That I should despise the things of this world, and seek with my heart the things that are above. The earth is continually in motion, the heavens are at rest. Here I find little but care, and trouble, and agitation; there I shall enter into rest. That which the earth yields is transitory; it is ever passing from one to another; today it is mine, to-morrow it is the property of another: the blessings of heaven are eternal. He who dwelleth there, is without variableness or shadow of turning. I will seek to be like St. Paul—the earth behind, heaven before me, myself in the midst, and "forgetting those things which are behind, and reaching forth unto those things which are before, I press toward the mark for the prize of the high calling of God in Christ Jesus," Phil. 3:13, 14. I will follow the guidance of my Savior, that I may dwell with him in heaven for ever.

THE PEACEMAKER

"MINE, and thine," said a heathen philosopher, "is the cause of all strife." I say, on the other hand, that mine and thine, on the principles of the gospel, putteth an end to strife.

Is God displeased with me on account of my sins, and ready to summon me to judgment? I approach him in the name of another, and receive pardon and grace. Blessed Jesus, my sins are thine. Thou hast taken them to thyself, that they may be washed away in thy blood. Thy righteousness is my righteousness, that I may be accepted in thee. What, therefore, can justice find in me? Can it find sin? It can find none; all my sins are laid on Jesus. "Himself took our infirmities, and bare our sicknesses," Matt. 8:17. Can it find righteousness? That I possess in Christ. "In the Lord have I righteousness and strength," Isa. 45:24.

Is Satan enraged against me? Thine and mine must divide us from each other. "Thine," I say to him, "is hell; mine is heaven. Keep thine own, leave to me mine, and then shall we both have our own."

Does death threaten me? I fear him not, but say to him, "Let us make an exchange; give me that which is thine, and take mine. I will give you my weariness, give me your rest. I will give you my sorrows, give me your joys."

With you, also, my brother, will I not contend. We are brethren, let us be of one mind. Thine and mine shall adjust every difference. You are as rich as I; I am as rich as you. God is thine, he is mine also. He is thy Father, and my Father. Jesus is mine, he is thine also—my brother and thy brother. Heaven is mine, it is thine also—thine inheritance and my inheritance.

Do I possess wealth, honor, and worldly estimation, let it not disturb you. They are neither mine nor thine. God gives them to whom he will. I possess as though I possessed not. Today they are mine, to-morrow thine. You may perhaps have to-morrow what I have today. You may be to-morrow what I am today. Have you little and I much? No more belongs to me of my abundance, than to you of your poverty. Let us be one—thou mine, I thine—one heart and one soul.

THE

REPENTANT PUBLICAN

I FIND five marks of wisdom in the poor publican. His prayer is short, but who can utter it from the heart without tears? "God be merciful to me a sinner," Luke 18:31.

1. *He approaches God as a sinner.* We are separated from God by sin; we return to him by repentance. Can you put fire and straw together, without the straw being consumed? And is not God a consuming fire? and are not sinners as chaff or stubble? But faith brings us near to God; it makes us know of his love to a fallen world, and his desire to save it.

2. *He speaks of mercy in connection with his sins.* Yet mercy and sin are opposed to each other. But faith builds on the promises of grace which are addressed to the penitent, and appropriates them to itself.

3. *He interposes grace between God and himself.* "God he merciful to me a sinner." The sword is drawn to take vengeance on the sinner, but grace averts the blow. Between an angry God and a weeping penitent, grace stands forth with words of comfort. Let not your works stand between you and your God, for with them you merit death. In yourself you can find nothing which can atone for sin; therefore, rejecting self, look only to the mercy of God.

4. The fourth mark of wisdom in the prayer of the publican is, that *he seeks the mercy of God only in Christ.* "For his sake, whom thou hast set forth to be a propitiation, through faith in his name, forgive me my sins." This is intimated in the original, ἱλάσθητι. None of us deserve mercy; it is the fruit of the love of God in Christ Jesus. Receive Christ, and you receive mercy and grace in him. When you point in faith to the wounds of Jesus, God cannot

but save you. Believe, therefore, in Christ. Cleave to him. Are you sinful in yourself? in him you have righteousness? Are you in yourself under condemnation and death? you possess life and salvation in him. He can pay more than you owe. One drop of his blood is sufficient to cleanse from sin the whole world, as well as yourself.

5. The fifth and last point to be observed is *the close connection which subsists between confession and absolution.* "God be merciful to me a sinner." The confession is full, the blessing sought is large. I say, "I am a poor sinner;" what will God do to me? Reject me he will not; his mercy forbids it; much more, his oath. Hath he not said, "As I live, saith the Lord God, I have no pleasure in the death of the wicked; but that the wicked turn from his way and live?" Ezek. 33:11. God cannot but answer me, "I will be merciful unto thee." Oh, yes; on earth right goes for grace; grace for right in heaven. There is always grace and mercy in God for a sinner. God himself hasteneth to meet him, embraceth him in the arms of mercy, and saith, "Return, thou backsliding Israel, and I will not cause mine anger to fall upon you: for I am merciful, saith the Lord, and I will not keep anger forever," Jer. 3:12. Therefore I venture; I return with the prodigal son, and exclaim, "Father, I have sinned against heaven, and in thy sight, and am no more worthy to be called thy son," Luke 15:21. He will be merciful unto me. I know it well.

ON

PERSECUTING THE CHILDREN OF GOD

YOU hate and persecute the believer. I do not wonder. He is an Abel, and you are a Cain, with the spirit of Cain, which is that of a murderer. How can those love, who have not the spirit of love? Men seek in vain for figs on thorns, or sweetness in the sea, or love in him, who rages in wrath and bitterness against the godly. But tell me, whom do you most injure? Yourself, or them? Scarcely have you stretched forth your hand against their goods or their persons, before you have wounded your own soul. Whoever rushes into a fire, or dashes himself against a rock, is a fool, and hurts nothing but himself. The righteous hath a wall of fire round about him, and hath built his house upon a rock. If a man endeavor to extinguish a torch with his hand, he causes, indeed, some little obscurity at first, but the flame soon bursts forth the more brightly, and he has only blackened or burnt his hand. You injure not the child of God by persecution, but do him a service. His humility, gentleness, long-suffering, and patience, are thus exercised and augmented, and his heavenly crown is rendered more bright and glorious. Yourself, however, you injure; you become more restless, malicious, and hard-hearted, and will, at length, bring yourself to shame. Believers should be had in honor; they are the children of God; they speak to him with the freedom and confidence of friends; they have power with God, and stand in the gap. Doth God visit a land in judgment to destroy it, they hasten to meet him, fall down before him, and appease his wrath.

Do men persecute the righteous, they cause God to withdraw from them, and there is no more certain sign of approaching ruin. Sodom persecuted Lot; Lot departed thence; Sodom was destroyed. Israel went out of Egypt, when they could no longer endure the oppression under which they groaned; and Pharaoh, with his chariots and his horsemen, were drowned in the Red Sea. How great a treasure and a blessing are the righteous in the land! Did not Joseph save the whole of Egypt in a time of famine? Did not Moses interpose for the preservation of the people, when God was about to destroy them utterly in the wilderness? But the righteous are a treasure hidden in a field, which no men regard, since no man knows of it, and it is trodden under foot.

It is a mark of great blindness, that men persecute the righteous, who receive power and protection from the brute creation, and even from inanimate nature. The Red Sea divided into two parts, to let the children of Israel go through when Pharaoh and his hosts were purposing to destroy them. The lions spared Daniel when he was cast into their den to be devoured. The ravens fed Elijah, whom Jezebel would have left to perish with hunger. The great fish received Jonah, whom the sailors had cast into the sea. The flames protected, as by an encircling wall, the young men whom Nebuchadnezzar had cast into the burning fiery furnace. I will studiously avoid persecuting the righteous, for in so doing, I seek to injure whole cities and nations, and even God himself; and should I be persecuted, I will bear it patiently.

The more Pharaoh oppressed the children of Israel, the more they prospered and increased. Joseph was persecuted by his brethren, and was elevated thereby to great honor. What injury can the wickedness of the world inflict upon me, when God is the strength of my heart and my portion forever? Can the thorns hurt the roses, or the fire the gold? No man can suffer harm, except from his own heart.

ON
READING THE BIBLE

YOU boast that you have read the Bible through many times. The reading is good—the boast is of no value. The profit is yours, the praise should be given to God. "Not unto us, O Lord, not unto us, but unto thy name, give glory," Psalm 115:1.

Love the Bible, and read it; it is a costly treasure, more precious than gold. "The law of thy mouth," saith David, "is better unto me than thousands of gold and silver," Psa. 119:72. Are you in the broad way? It, by the power of the Spirit, guides your steps into the narrow way which leadeth unto life, and surrounds your path with the doctrine and life of Jesus. Are you in doubt and error? It sheds upon you its sacred light, and dispels the darkness. Does your heart tend to the world? It draws it back. The fire of the word consumes worldly lusts. When it communicates to you a lively sense of the love of God, it soon expels the love of the world. It attracts the heart as a magnet, to heaven, when our natural corruption would press us to the ground. Is the heart indisposed to that which is good? The Bible draws it to God by the manifestation of his goodness and mercy. Are not such allurements of love calculated to soften the hard heart, or warm the cold heart? Such power doth the goodness of God possess, when it is carried home to the heart; it draws it with such a sweet and mighty influence, that the heart delights to do that which would be pleasing to God. Are you sorrowful? The Bible comforts you; for it is the voice of a gracious God, whose love is beyond that of a mother, and whose words cannot but be consoling to his weeping child. Are you weak? He strengthens you. His word is as a cordial to your fainting soul.

But, my friend, read not the Bible as a mere historical book, that your mind may be furnished with the knowledge of its contents, but that your heart may be affected; that your devotion may be excited, and that the power of the word may be manifested in your life. The Bible is not designed to make you clever, but holy; not to give you the spirit of disputants, but to fill your heart with love. The devil showed, by the temptation in the wilderness, that he knew the Bible, yet not for his own profit, but for the purpose of tempting therewith Christ and his members. Many learned disputants study the Bible very diligently, not for their own improvement, but in order to perplex others.

The word of God shall be to me a glass, in which, under the teaching of the Holy Spirit, I behold what I was in Adam before the fall, what I became by the fall, what I am in Christ, and shall be in eternity. The first, by God's grace, will excite in me love to God, and to repentance, which proceeds from love; the second will work in me self-condemnation, the mortification of the flesh, humility, gentleness, and patience; the third will implant in me faith and godly fear; the fourth will teach me to despise the vanities of time, and to aspire after an eternity of blessedness.

ON

TRUE HUMILITY OF SOUL

"THE Lord seeth not as man seeth; for man looketh on the outward appearance, but the Lord looketh on the heart," 1 Sam. 16:7. Men judge of the poverty or wealth, the dignity or lowliness of others, by outward things; God sees their hearts, and estimates them according to the manner in which they think and feel in their various circumstances. What benefit is it if I am poor and needy, and yet discontented? None whatever. Again, what disadvantage was it to the holy patriarchs, Abraham, Isaac, and Jacob, that they were rich? What harm did the royal throne do to David, or his high dignity and power in Babylon to Daniel, if their hearts were not given to earthly greatness, and their treasure therein? There must necessarily be external distinctions in persons and stations upon earth, but the heart must not be involved in them; it should neither be set on riches, nor averse to poverty; it should neither love greatness, nor dread the low estate of the poor. It is no humility before God to wear mean apparel, or associate with your inferiors, that you may be regarded by men as humble; yea, I ask you, whether your heart is not aspiring after great things, which you hope to attain through this very show of humility? The man who is really humble, is quite different; he affects no studied abasement. As the spring of water flows from the fountain, so are the manifestations of his humility simple and unpremeditated. Honor unsought followeth such a man, and his elevation taketh place unexpectedly, for his desire is to serve God in the state in which he is, without looking for a higher place. But he who falsely assumes the garb of humility, wonders that his honor and advancement are so tardy in their approach, for his natural pride spurns his present abasement, in which he finds no pleasure, and he is ever reaching after something beyond. In a word, true humility knows not that it is humble.

How wonderful was the salutation of the angel to the Virgin Mary! How amazed was she at the tidings of the honor designed her! for she had not thought it possible that such distinguished favor should be shown unto her. On the other hand, assumed humility never knows that it is proud.

Oh, let us prove ourselves, and seek to follow more simply the footsteps of Jesus, who was "meek and lowly in heart." For this we must learn of him, and we shall thus have peace in our souls, Matt. 11:29.

ON THE

DELIVERANCE GOD EFFECTS FOR HIS PEOPLE

THE snare is broken, and I am delivered. Thank God, I yet live! When the knife was already held to the throat of Isaac, God interposed.

"As chastened, and not killed," 2 Cor. 6:9. When the enemy approaches us with some evil intention, the Lord restrains him; "You may chasten my child," he says, "but not destroy him; you may be his physician, but not his murderer." The world abounds in enemies bent on our ruin. How full of violence is man to his fellow man! were it possible, he would call fire down from heaven to consume him. But however malignant he is to destroy, God is powerful to deliver. How wonderfully has He defeated the machinations of the enemies of his church, and preserved her even unto this day, as a bird escaped from the snare of the fowler! What an amazing deliverance was that effected at the Red Sea; and again at the city of Jerusalem, when no enemy could shoot an arrow against it! How was the power of God manifested in behalf of the prophet Elisha, when encompassed by the hosts of the Syrians in Dothan; and of St. Paul, when beset by the Jews, who thirsted for his blood; and of St. Peter, when in prison, and about to be brought forth thence and put to death! Dioclesian and Maximin had vowed utterly to extinguish the light of Christianity. But of what avail? They both came to a fearful end. Therefore, let not your heart be troubled, neither let it be afraid. The enemy spreads forth his net; his murderous purposes are unknown to you. Unconsciously you are entangled in the snare. They cry at once, "He is now in our power." But "He that sitteth in the heavens shall laugh" them to scorn: "the Lord shall have them in derision," Psa. 2:4. Before the net can be closed, the imprisoned one hath escaped. God is faithful, and to them that wait on him, he will cause every trial to terminate for their good. Those that wait on him shall not be ashamed, Psa. 25:3. Is not the enemy often entrapped in his own snares, and pierced with his own sword? Many a one falls into the pit which he had digged for another, and draws upon himself the evil which he proposed to inflict. God giveth not his people unto the will of their enemies. He knoweth how to deliver the righteous, and to repay to the ungodly their wicked imaginations. How often has the persecutor thought that his victim was within his grasp, but God has, beyond all expectation, manifested himself in behalf of his child. Praised be his name for evermore. Amen.

ON THE

UNCERTAINTY OF DEATH

DEATH is certain. As we all have entered upon life, so must we depart hence. He who doubts of the certainty of death, knows not that he is dying daily. The moment our life commences we begin to die, and we continue dying as our life advances. As the wine is not at once expressed from the grapes, but drop by drop, so it is with our life, till the last particle is gone. But the hour of death is uncertain. You look forward to old age, and rejoice in the glory of your youth. All are not strong enough to sustain the weight of age; all are not honored with grey hairs, which are a crown of glory, when found in the paths of righteousness, Prov. 16:31. Death tells you not first when he will come; in a moment he thrusts in his sickle, and you are cut down; you are never too unripe for his barn.

When Jezebel has painted her face, and attired her hair, she is immediately to be thrown down, and eaten by the dogs. When Belshazzar is feasting amid the splendors of his court, and drinking wine out of the golden goblets, death is portrayed upon his wall. When the rich fool is saying to himself, "Soul, thou hast much goods laid up for many years; take thine ease, eat, drink, and be merry," those awful words are sounded in his ears, "Thou fool, this night thy soul shall be required of thee," Luke 12:19, 20. Look not, therefore, far forward. Be not careful for the morrow, perhaps you may die today. He who gave you your life today, gave you with it the means of subsistence. Should he add to you another day, he will provide for you the bread that is needful. Think not to repent to-morrow, it may be too late; today is, perhaps, your last day. This night you may die. "Truly as the Lord liveth, and as thy soul liveth," said David to Jonathan, "there is but a step between me and death," 1 Sam. 20:3. You may say the same also; whether at home, or abroad, whether journeying, or at rest, death is ever to be expected. Are you on shipboard? There is scarcely a plank between you and death. Are you on horseback? A fall may terminate your life. Are you walking in the street? A tile from a roof may cut short your days. Our life is only a handbreadth, yea, it is even as nothing. Death shall, if it please God, not come to me unexpectedly; I will look for it every hour.

"He which testifieth these things saith, Surely, I come quickly; amen. Even so, come, Lord Jesus," Rev. 22:20.

ON

THE IMPROVEMENT OF EARLY HOURS

IF every morning it rained gold, many would rise early to collect it. Yet he who is early at his work receives his gold at the right time. By frequent digging men at length discover the vein of precious metal. Labor rests on a golden ground. But what advantage do you reap from much wealth? It is given in this life, and taken away in the same. It comes from the earth, and returns to it again. Here it is found, and here lost.

But let us trace riches to their true source. They come from God. If I have God, I have wealth enough. His blessing maketh rich. If I have God, I have that which is better than gold. When wealth takes to itself wings and flies away, God remains. Gold is always a dumb idol. It can neither counsel nor comfort, when counsel or comfort is needed. God draws near to me with counsel, when all is dark and confused around me; he speaks to me in comfort, when the water goeth even over my soul. Wealth lays on me a burden of care; God enables me to cast my care on him, seeing he careth for me. You may covet wealth, I will delight in God. To Him they brought, under the Old Testament, the firstlings of their cattle, and of the first-fruits of the ground. I present to him the first-fruits of my days. God thinketh of me early, and his goodness is renewed every morning. I will think of him early, and every morning offer unto him the calves of my lips; even thanksgivings unto his name. He hath protected me in the night watches, when I have laid me down and slept. He hath kept me in safety, as under the shadow of his wings, and no enemy has come nigh me; no misfortune has befallen me. Therefore, I present unto him my morning sacrifice of praise and thanksgiving. It is my daily earnest supplication that he would direct me by his Spirit; that he would keep me from sin and evil; that he would bless my labor, and help me to bear my cross. Should he send no temporal success, yet He still remains, and having him, I possess all things. When I am hungry, he supports me; when oppressed, he comforts me; when sorrowful, he gives me joy. "Whom have I in heaven but thee? and there is none upon earth that I desire besides thee. My flesh and my heart faileth: but God is the strength of my heart, and my portion forever," Psa. 73:26. My happiness is in God. Let yours be in him also.

ON THE

JUDGMENT OF GOD AGAINST THE PERSECUTOR

BE still, and wait upon the Lord. In quietness and confidence is the Christian's strength. Why does not the world experience the wondrous help of God? Is it not, that they cannot be still and wait for it? If any man would hurt them, they rage, fret, and contend, and defend their own cause, taking it out of the hand of God. Jesus was falsely accused before Pilate, but he answered not a word. And what did God do? He put these liars to shame. Their testimony agreed not with each other. If the matter is God's, he desireth not human interference. Should man be God's advocate and defender? The God of heaven will stop the mouth of wickedness by his judgments. The adversary and accuser would not cease to assault and calumniate, if men had no means of defense upon earth. "Thou didst cause judgment to be heard from heaven," says Asaph; "the earth feared, and was still, when God arose to judgment, to save all the meek of the earth. Surely the wrath of man shall praise thee; the remainder of wrath shalt thou restrain," Psa. 76:8–10. Think of the end of Pharaoh, Saul, Ahab, Jezebel, and Herod. It is the cause of God. As long as God is silent, the calumniator and persecutor go forth in the pride and haughtiness of their hearts; they encourage each other in their wickedness. Satan is then alert. If God speak but one word, they are checked. Whilst Jesus slept, the waves raged, and the winds were tempestuous; but as soon as he rebuked the winds and the waves, they were still; there was a great calm. If the enemy become so desperate in his folly as to assail Christ and his gospel, there is no cause of fear. Though we may receive injury from men, we have, nevertheless, honor from God. Whatsoever respects the honor of the Savior, no man can touch. The gates of hell cannot prevail against this rock. But you say, My good name, in the mean time, suffers injury. But how long? Does not David say, "Commit thy way unto the Lord; trust also in him; and he shall bring it to pass. And he shall bring forth thy righteousness as the light, and thy judgment as the noonday," Psa. 37:5, 6. It was nearly ten years that David was pursued by Saul, but Saul, with all his power, could not prevail against him. God brought him forward at length as a beautiful light; and how brilliantly did that light shine throughout the whole land. A great eclipse obscured, for a time, Joseph, and Daniel; but in due time God brought them forth out of the darkness: and Joseph shone in Egypt, and Daniel in Persia, with more splendor than the sun in the heavens.

Should I be persecuted, I will spread my complaint before God. He hath forbidden me to avenge myself. Vengeance belongeth unto him, he will repay. The cause is his; and no less the recompense upon the transgressors. He hath sustained me hitherto, and given me honor. How many holy men has he moved to defend me, partly by their discourses, partly by their pen, against the voice of calumny! Be still, therefore, and know that he is God. His wrath upon the transgressor comes slowly, but falls heavily.

ON

CHRISTIAN CONSTANCY

IN war he obtains the most praise who continues on the field of battle to the last. Our life is a scene of warfare. Are not men compelled to live in continual strife? Accustom, then, your heart to firmness, and be not the first to give way. Your flesh warreth against you, and its strength consists in the fleshly lusts and desires which war against the soul. Your strength consists in forbearance.

The flesh moves your members to serve unrighteousness, from one degree of iniquity to another; your mouth to speak that which is evil; your hand to oppress, and so forth. Consent not thereto. Should the flesh proceed with its allurements and enticements, repel it with firmness in the name of the Lord. Be the last on the field. When you have to bear your cross, you are sometimes reluctant, and would fain be excused. Be not so; you must not be weary and unwilling to bear the cross; patience will make it light. It avails not to give way; to persevere is to succeed. Be resolved in God's strength to sustain the utmost extremity of suffering and distress, rather than to yield in the conflict. Firmness and constancy will then be crowned with victory; but cowardice and timidity are succeeded by a fall.

Satan assaults you with his fiery darts. And how do you act? Do you retreat? He seizes you from behind, and you become an easy prey; nor will he soon relinquish his hold. It is better to withstand him in the name of the Lord. "Whom resist," says St. Peter, "steadfast in the faith," 1 Pet. 5:9. Your ground is the word of God. To that word continue steadfast to the last, like Jesus in the wilderness. "It is written," exclaim again and again. Then must the devil depart with shame and disgrace.

Death also will draw near in battle. But he cannot inflict a deadly wound upon the Christian. He was deprived of his sting in the garden of Gethsemane, and on the mount of Olives by the Captain of our salvation. Meet him, therefore, with confidence, recollecting your high privilege as a member of Christ, and say, "Christ is my life; to die is gain."

And if, at any time, you should appear to be forsaken of your God, cease not to seek him when he hideth himself, until you find him. He cannot continue to conceal himself when you search for him with earnest longings of soul, and with tears. Hath not the Lord said by the prophet Jeremiah, and doth not his word continue sure? "I know the thoughts that I think towards you, saith the Lord, thoughts of peace, and not of evil, to give you an expected end. Then shall ye call upon me, and ye shall go and pray unto me, and I will hearken unto you. And ye shall seek me, and find me, when ye shall search for me with all your heart," Jer. 29:11–13. Do you say with Hezekiah, "I reckoned till morning, that, as a lion, so will he break all my bones: from day even to night wilt thou make an end of me. Mine eyes fail with looking upward," Isa. 38:13, 14. Remember his mercy towards that servant of the Lord; forget not that he is your Father; that he chastens, but means not to destroy, and that his dealings with you are love. Say with Jacob, when wrestling with the Angel, "I will not let thee go, except thou bless me," Gen. 32:26. The crown awaits the victor. Be more than conquerors through Him that has loved you. Hear the words of the Savior himself, "Be thou faithful unto death, and I will give thee a crown of life," Rev. 2:10. I will, the Lord being my helper.

ON THE

STRENGTH OF GOD MADE PERFECT IN WEAKNESS

THE world says that the strongest shall prevail, and therefore powerful men associate together for the purposes of war. But what is the power of man without the help of God! God delighteth in giving power to the weak. How much attention does a mother pay to her sick child, and a shepherd to the most feeble lambs of his flock! God regards us with yet greater tenderness, and can as little forget us as a mother can forget her child. He is our Shepherd, and he carries us in his arms, yea, near to his heart.

He careth for us, especially when we are weak and destitute. The oppressed, especially, have need to open the door of their hearts to God, that he may confer on them comforts, of which others know nothing. Adam and Eve both sinned, and yet it was Eve that was comforted, and not her husband. She was in greater affliction; since she had led her husband into the transgression, and, as a woman, her strength was less to sustain the assaults of hell. As the enemy is wont to direct his attacks against the weakest, so doth God especially stand ready for his help. "My strength," he saith, "is made perfect in weakness," 2 Cor. 12:9. Were the strength of God put forth in behalf of the strong, he would have to share with them the honor; but he alone will bear the glory. "Not unto us, O Lord, not unto us, but unto thy name be the praise," Psa. 115:1.

If there be strength of our own, then is there, for the most part, self-idolatry: man is then prone to trust more to himself and his own strength, than to God. How can God be the God of him who is his own god, and looks to himself for help? God will unite himself only to such a heart as altogether denies that it has power of its own, and trusts simply to him, saying with Jehoshaphat, "We have no might against this great company that cometh against us; neither know we what to do: but our eyes are upon thee; and in thine hand is there not power and might, so that none is able to withstand thee?" 2 Chron. 20:12, 6. How much does a sick child look to its mother, and depend on her kind aid. Even so should the soul cleave unto the Lord, saying, "O my God, my Savior, my faithful God, thou canst and wilt help me!" Then doth God give power and strength for war. Be not, therefore, distressed that you are weak. Though you may suppose that God is farthest from you when you are weak, yet be assured that he is even then nearest at hand. When God leaves his children under their trials to become so powerless that men think they are forsaken, they have, nevertheless, at that very time, the greatest strength, though it is so hidden and concealed, that the sufferers themselves do not feel it, but only believe that it is so. For, where the strength of man ends, there the power of God begins; yet it is not ordinarily made manifest till the trial has become great: then man first becomes conscious of the strength which was made perfect in his weakness. On the other hand, God permits the enemies of his church to become great and mighty; but frequently when their power and their boasting have attained their greatest height, he brings them to nothing. "The fool knoweth not," says Luther, "that when he riseth up in his supposed strength, he is rejected of God; and that, when his time is come, he will he utterly destroyed."

I will be of good courage under my trials, for the weaker I am in myself, the stronger am I in my God. Should Satan assault me, I fear him not. I go forth against him in the strength of the Lord God of sabaoth. By the help of my God, I can do valiantly. Should it be said, The stronger will gain the victory; then the victory is already mine: for the strength of God is my strength, and it is over all. Should it be said, The weaker shall prevail; then shall I prevail, for such am I in myself. Blessed be the name of the Lord, I shall yet enjoy peace and rest, and shall come off more than conqueror, through Him that hath loved me.

THE

CHRISTIAN IN NAME ONLY.—CHRIST AND ANTICHRIST

THE voice of Jacob and the hands of Esau—so great is the difference between the name and the reality. "He that is not with me," saith our Lord, "is against me," Matt. 12:30. If you are a Christian, you are "with Christ." You are united to him by faith; he is the Bridegroom, you are the bride; he is the Husband, you are the wife. You follow him as a partaker of spiritual life; and are found with him in the only way, the narrow way, which leadeth to life eternal. You would not forsake him in the path of sorrow, but cheerfully accompany him to sufferings and to death, and say, with St. Paul, "Who shall separate us from the love of Christ? shall tribulation, or distress, or persecution, or famine, or nakedness, or peril, or sword? As it is written, For thy sake we are killed all the day long; we are accounted as sheep for the slaughter. Nay, in all these things we are more than conquerors through him that loved us. For I am persuaded, that neither death, nor life, nor angels, nor principalities, nor powers, nor things present, nor things to come, nor height, nor depth, nor any other creature, shall be able to separate us from the love of God, which is in Christ Jesus our Lord," Rom. 8:35–39.

Dost thou abide with Jesus? then art thou never forsaken. O happy souls who are thus with Christ! Let a storm or tempest arise, He is a "refuge from the storm, a shadow from the heat, when the blast of the terrible ones is as a storm against the wall," Isa. 25:4. Should the enemy, as a roaring lion, fall upon them, and seek to devour them, they flock to the Savior, as sheep to their shepherd, and find in him the protection which they need. The children of God betake themselves to him, and become, through his grace, rich in good works. They lay up treasures in heaven. Their sighs and tears are had in remembrance. Since they are with Christ, he also is with them; their light in darkness, their fullness in want, their riches in poverty, their refuge in distress, their comfort in trouble, their joy in sorrow. What more can they desire? Tell me, are they not happy?

But, alas, how few such are there among those that are called Christians! The larger proportion, it is to be feared, are antichristian. They are "against Christ." They oppose the doctrine of Christ, and deem it foolishness; they reject his word; they calumniate and persecute his faithful ministers, who show to them the way to heaven; they deny Christ in their lives. He was holy, and full of love, and gentleness, and humility, and patience; they are unholy, full of hatred and wrath, pride and impatience. Ah, who can say it without weeping? Christ and his holy life are entirely lost among those who are called Christians. The dissipated, sumptuous, fashionable course of the world pleases them better than the strict and lowly life of Jesus. Under the cross they fall away from Christ: they forsake him with Demas; they deny him with Peter. They "desire to make a fair show in the flesh, only lest they should suffer persecution for the cross of Christ," Gal. 6:12. Yes, when Jesus weeps, they laugh; when he walks through thorns, they recline among roses; they oppress the oppressed, and trouble the troubled yet more. Are they Christians? Yes, if a wolf is a sheep, and a serpent is a dove. They are antichrist, enemies of Christ. And how numerous they are! They are enough to make one's heart weep blood. O wretched men! They are scattered abroad, and as wandering sheep they have become a prey to the wicked one. They have forsaken Jesus, and he has let them alone. Where can they find a refuge, or counsel, or comfort when they have need?

I will cleave to Jesus, and he will keep me as the apple of his eye. If he be with me, who can be against me? If he be with me, a hundred thousand devils cannot hurt even a hair of my head.

ON THE

FREEDOM OF THE BELIEVER

"I OWE you nothing; why do you make a demand of me?" Thus I boldly speak to Moses, when he opens his book, and requires to be paid his due. I am united to Christ. He hath himself said, "I will betroth thee unto me forever; yea, I will betroth thee unto me in righteousness, and in judgment, and in loving-kindness, and in mercies. I will even betroth thee unto me in faithfulness; and thou shalt know the Lord," Hosea 2:19, 20. I am his bride; he is the Bridegroom. No man can sue the wife by law; her husband is answerable. When Moses therefore calls me to account, I point him to Christ, and say, "I owe you nothing; why do you make a demand of me? Behold my Husband! he will answer for me. *I* am required no more to give satisfaction to the law for my transgressions, but Christ himself; since through faith I have laid hold of his strength, I have received his atonement, and made it my own. Christ is justified, that is, set free from our sins, and I am justified in him. For, "there is now no condemnation to them which are in Christ Jesus, who walk not after the flesh, but after the Spirit," Rom. 8:1. I have perfectly fulfilled the law in my Surety, and paid the uttermost farthing, since the satisfaction of Christ is mine. Would it not be unrighteous if a crime were twice atoned for, and a debt twice paid? The law cannot condemn me. I appeal to the gospel. The gospel cannot condemn me, for I believe in Jesus Christ, and obtain through faith this verdict, "He that believeth shall be saved," Mark 16:16. My conscience may be my accuser, and so may Moses, and so may Satan; but my Judge cannot. I triumph with St. Paul, "Who shall separate us from the love of God?" Rom. 8:35. Is not God he who justifies? Is not Christ he who died? Let but the Judge acquit me, I care not for the accuser. My salvation or destruction is not in the power of the accuser, but of the Judge. But how can the Judge condemn me when he hath given *himself* for me? His blood is sufficient for ten thousand sinful worlds; and sooner must He himself be condemned, than that those sins for which he hath made atonement can be followed by condemnation and death. It is to faith in his blood I owe it that I am strong, and not easily moved from my hope. The foundation on which I build can never be moved. The Rock of ages ever endures. Oh what a strong confidence, what a steadfast hope shall I thus possess when Satan comes and accuses me in the last hour. "Get thee hence, Satan," I will say; "whosoever believeth in Christ can never be condemned; he hath fulfilled all righteousness in the person of Christ, and is declared free!" Well! but how then did the servant in the parable say, "I will pay thee all?" Matt. 18:26. We may say it with reference to our Surety. He hath fulfilled all righteousness. He hath kept the whole law, and paid the uttermost farthing of our debt. Praised be his name! It is written on my heart. It is all my salvation, and all my desire. He is all my comfort and joy, my all in all.

ON THE

SOCIETY OF THE UNGODLY

ONE misleads the other. Look well before you. The foot leads the eye, the eye the heart, and the heart the head. When Achan confessed his sin, he said, "When I *saw* among the spoils a goodly Babylonish garment, and two hundred shekels of silver, and a wedge of gold of fifty shekels weight, then I *coveted* them, and *took* them," Josh. 7:21. He omits to specify the foot, which was, however, his first seducer. Had Eve stated the order of the temptation and sin, this, no doubt, would have been the nature of her confession, "I went to the tree, I beheld the fruit, I desired it, and took it." This is the usual course in all sin. The foot conducts us to the forbidden tree, the eye is attracted, the heart longs for it, the hand plucks the fruit, and the transgression is complete. The foot takes us into the society of the ungodly, there the eye sees that which is evil, the heart becomes inflamed, and arms our own hand against us to the commission of sin. The best counsel is to avoid such company. Had Peter remained out of the palace of the high-priest he might not have denied his Lord. His presumptuous foot was the first transgressor. Whoever warms himself at the fire of the ungodly must with them persecute Christ. How evil was it in Jehoshaphat to join himself with that wicked Ahaz! It nearly cost him his life, whilst it laid him under the Divine displeasure. "Wherefore," said the seer to king Jehoshaphat, "shouldest thou help the ungodly, and love them that hate the Lord? therefore is wrath upon thee from the Lord," 2 Chron. 19:2. If the ungodly bear with your company, it is to be feared that you are like-minded with them. The physician visits his patient as long as there is hope of doing him service, but when that hope is lost, he gives him up. As long as you can entertain a good hope of turning the ungodly from their wicked ways, you may use your best efforts to gain them; but when the fear and danger of your being ensnared by their evil courses, is greater than the hope of their recovery, it is time for you to withdraw, and not knowingly continue in a perilous situation; that you may not encourage them in their wickedness, or offend those whose consciences are weak.

I will keep my feet that I go not into the society of the ungodly; but should I, from necessity, be brought into his company, I will, by God's grace, guard against the injury I might receive, and will do my endeavor to benefit his soul.

ON

THE CHRISTIAN'S RULE OF CONDUCT

HOW seldom does man inquire after what is right! He seeks rather that which will yield some pleasure, honor, or profit. Let not these, my friend, be the objects of your desire. That which appears advantageous to the body, may be most injurious to the soul. And what would you be profited if you gained the whole world, and lost your own soul? Godliness is alone profitable, having the promise of the life that now is, and of that which is to come. With contentment it is great gain.

Ask not for glory and renown. That which is highly esteemed by the world is an abomination unto the Lord. Would you attain honor, be the servant of Christ, for His promise is sure: "If any man serve me, him will my Father honor," John 12:26. How can the world communicate that which is good, when the whole world lieth in wickedness? If you participate in her sins, you must endure her plagues. If your neighbor rush into the flames, must you then madly follow him? In all your undertakings be this your constant inquiry, "Is it right?" Men often mistake their duty. "Say we not well," said the Jews to Christ, "that thou art a Samaritan, and hast a devil?" John 8:48; see also verses 44 and 52. They put darkness for light, and light for darkness. Their self-love blinded them. Put, therefore, to your conscience this question, "Is it right?" "For if our heart condemn us, God is greater than our heart, and knoweth all things," 1 John 3:20. The word of God, under the teaching of the Spirit of God, and your conscience rightly instructed thereby, must he the rule of all your actions: that which is according to this rule is right. St. Paul would have you "prove what is that good, and acceptable, and perfect will of God," Rom. 12:2.

Many easily satisfy themselves; they deem that to be the will of God which their own inclination, or an enticing world, sets forth as such. Let it not be so with you; but prove it. A jeweller does not think everything gold which bears its similitude; but he weighs it, and tries it on a stone. Your test of duty is the word of God, which he hath given to instruct and direct you in all things, and, under the teaching of his Spirit, you shall understand it aright. Whatsoever is His will, that do in the name of God. Heed not the frown of man.

The word of God shall be my rule, by which I will ever seek to walk, for then I cannot go astray.

ON

TRUE CHRISTIAN ZEAL

IN fire there is both light and warmth. Zeal is like fire, and in it wisdom and love should be united. How dangerous is fire in the hand of a fool! More dangerous is zeal without knowledge. Mistaken zeal, through excess of passion, often brings discredit on the truth which it should protect. St. Paul's spirit was greatly moved within him, when he beheld the Ephesians wholly given to idolatry, as worshippers of the great goddess Diana, and her image, which came down from Jupiter; yet he singled her not out by name from among them, but remarked generally, that those were not gods that were made by the hands of men. Had he spoken to them more pointedly, he might, perhaps, have cast fire upon a train which would have destroyed the whole church of Christ in that city. Zeal is an earnest desire to accomplish a given object. If it be without wisdom, how can a man use the means requisite for such a purpose? A wise man considers not only, what it is his duty to do, but how he can do it aright. By this test St. Paul tried the zeal of the Jews, and found it to be, not according to knowledge. They had a zeal for God, but of such a nature, that they became the murderers of his only begotten Son, and persecuted his disciples even unto death, as the Lord had forewarned them, "They shall put you out of the synagogues: yea, the time cometh, that whosoever killeth you will think that he doeth God service," John 16:2. There are those who in the darkness of their minds are zealous against Christ. Christ is to them antichrist, light is darkness, the truth is a lie and heresy. Pure zeal for Christ would not thus wound Christ and his servants as such men do with their murderous tongue. Wisdom should ever be associated with zeal, and both should he directed by love. Zeal without love, is not a warming and serviceable, but a consuming and injurious fire. Such was the zeal of the two disciples, when they would have called fire from heaven to consume the Samaritans.

Fire consumes, or separates, the dross, but leaves the gold uninjured. Our zeal should be directed against sin, not against the person of the sinner.

I will, through grace, so strive to be zealous for God, that I may not provoke him to be zealous against me.

ON

CHRISTIAN COURAGE

THE prophet Ezekiel was led through the holy waters, which were first to his ankles, afterwards to his knees, then to his loins, and lastly they were a river which he could not pass over, Ezek. 47:3–5. Thus are the waters of affliction seen to many a child of God. He fears not to venture into them when they are to the ankles, the knees, or even the loins; but he fears them beyond this; they are too deep; he can find no ground. If God bring him to the Red Sea, there he stands and trembles, ready to die. Alas! he exclaims, here I shall perish; I can never survive this. But this, my brother, is unworthy of your name and Christian character. You are commanded to go forward. He who brought you hither, will carry you onwards. Did he not make a passage through the sea? He knows how to make a path where none exists. Christian courage wades through every obstructing ford; and if we are led into the midst of the overwhelming floods, it will give us energy to buffet against the stream. It is a sore evil when a Christian's spirit fails in the midst of some trying providence, or when any opposing circumstance distresses him because he cannot see the end. We shall yet find ground. If Jesus go before me, I will follow after, and I cannot but be safe. If needful, he will support me by his arm. However deep the waters may be, the angels of God are with me, who will bear me up in their hands. I shall not sink beneath the flood, unless they sink also. It is as well to be in the deeps as on high, if only God and his angels are with me.

If one trial succeed another, it is not otherwise than I have been taught to expect. How many were the afflictions of my Savior? Did he not go out of Jerusalem to the Garden of Gethsemane, from Gethsemane to Annas, from Annas to

Caiaphas, from Caiaphas to Pilate, from Pilate to Herod, thence again to Pilate, and at last to Calvary, to be suspended on the accursed tree? Thus hath he sanctified to me the cross. Of what then should I be afraid? Is not my God and Savior near me? He who administered comforts to the Israelites in the wilderness, made also the Jordan dry. He will overrule all things for my good, and make those very circumstances which I most feared, conduce to my advantage. As I also, by his grace, trust him in the beginning, so shall I also, with him, in the end, be glorified. "I will trust, and not be afraid: for the Lord Jehovah is my strength and my song; he also is become my salvation," Isa. 12:2.

ON

CHRISTIAN CONTENTMENT

JOYS and sorrows frequently alternate. Luther has written very beautifully on this point:—"As God giveth his saints here on earth a foretaste of heavenly blessedness, so doth he permit them to feel some of the misery which is the portion of the lost. It was so with Joseph and the Virgin Mary. They had, indeed, in the birth of Jesus inexpressible joy when the shepherds came from the field of Bethlehem, and declared to them the message of the angel, and when the wise men from the east presented to the infant Jesus gold, frankincense, and myrrh. But how great was their anxiety when they had lost Jesus for three days. Thus was it also with the disciples. When Christ was with them, they had only joy. He even permitted some of them to behold his excellent glory on the holy mount; but when he was taken away from them, their hearts were full of anguish. And such is the experience of the children of God in our own day. Many are well pleased when their sky is bright, and all things are cheerful and smiling around them, but when thick clouds arise, and all is dark and dreary, their hearts are troubled. But it should not be so. If you love the hill of Tabor, you must not turn away from the mount of Olives. Your Savior is taking you with him. Sorrow is as salutary as joy; both are sent by the same God, and they are equally tokens of his love. In both he is deserving of your praise. "Shall we receive good at the hand of God, and shall we not receive evil?" Job 2:10. You say, "God hath hitherto fed me with the bread of comfort, how does he now send me the bread of tears to eat? Formerly I had the sweet experience of happiness in my prayers, how is it that my power for prayer, and my delight in a throne of grace, are now gone?"

My friend, it was not designed that you should be always a child. The young Christian God feeds with milk, and not with strong meat; he shows him many tokens of love, and holds him by the hand, teaching him to walk; but afterwards he would have him go alone, and confide in his Father's love, even when he corrects him with the rod, and appears more distant. Whilst you are crying for comforts, do you not manifest that you are still a babe? Those who are strong in Christy confide in the love of God under all circumstances; they are not more rejoiced in riches than in poverty, nor are they more sorrowful in shame than in honor, since God remains ever the same, equally as near when we are low, as when we are exalted.

I will be content with all the dispensations of my God. Do I love the giver? I will also fully acquiesce in his wisdom and love, and thankfully receive his gifts.

ON

THE DANGER OF FALLING

You say, "I am a Christian; I have nothing to fear." But on what is your confidence founded? Think not that profession is true faith. The word of God says, "Serve the Lord with fear, and rejoice with trembling," Psa. 2:11; and again, "Work out your own salvation with fear and trembling," Phil. 2:12. He that thinketh he standeth, should take heed lest he fall, 1 Cor. 10:12. Be mindful of your weakness, that you may not be suddenly overtaken of a fault; and let your eye ever be directed to Him who alone can keep you from falling. When you see any one fall, think of your own danger. Fear God, and walk circumspectly, that you may not transgress his word. Try yourself often, whether your heart is right with God, and you are walking in the narrow way. Should you at any time be overtaken by a fault, take heed that you love not the sin, nor continue in it, but go forth with Peter, and weep bitterly; betake yourself again to the blood of the covenant; the blood of sprinkling which speaketh better things than the blood of Abel. And let your prayer ascend unto God with earnestness, that he would graciously increase your faith, and render you more watchful in future, and more simply dependent on him, that he may uphold you with his right hand. Then may you express your confident persuasion, with St. Paul, that nothing shall be able to separate you from the love of God, which is in Christ Jesus our Lord, Rom. 8:39.

I will thus endeavor, by his grace, to keep myself; but should I fall, I will not cast away my confidence that God will raise me up again. I will go before him with a broken and a contrite heart, in the name of Jesus, and beseech him, for the sake of his well-beloved Son, to have mercy on me, and pardon my sin. I will not deem myself safe from the fear of evil, till I have fought the good fight, and kept the faith, and finished my course, and shall at length go to receive the crown of righteousness, which the Lord, the righteous Judge, shall give me in that day.

ON

LONGING AFTER HEAVEN

ON earth there is no *rest*. Can a little bark rest on the raging sea? As the earth is ever moving, so are all earthly things. The heart of man in his natural state is unquiet. Its desires are continually roaming in pursuit of fleeting vanities.

On earth there is no *security*. Woe unto the inhabitants of the earth, for the devil hath come down in great wrath, knowing that his time is short, Rev. 12:12. Is your heart set upon earthly things? Oh, how unsafe are you! How many souls has the devil thus entangled and caught in his snare!

On earth there is no *satisfaction*. What the world yields is imperfect, and is doled out in small portions to its deceived and discontented votaries. Look, therefore, my soul, beyond the earth and earthly things. Seek those things that are above.

In heaven there is *rest*. There HE dwells, whose heart is open to receive you, and who invites you in the most tender accents, "Come unto me, all ye that labor and are heavy laden, and I will give you rest," Matt. 11:28. There you will find *security*, for the devil is cast out, and will no more find admittance into heaven. In the spirits of the just made perfect, Satan has no part, nor can he do them any harm. There you will find *satisfaction*; you may now say with Asaph, "Whom have I in heaven but thee? God is my portion forever," Psa. 73:25, 26.

Look upwards, then, my soul; thy treasure is in heaven. All that the earth contains is too small for thee. As little can an atom of earth cover the whole expanse of the firmament, as the things of time fill the immortal soul. When that which is perfect is come, then that which is in part shall be done away. Let your thoughts, and affections, and desires, be above. Suffer not your heart to be weighed down by the cares and fears of this life. That is light which ascends upwards. Disburden yourself of earthly things, if you would enjoy those that are heavenly. Let the fire of love, of devotion, of holy meditation, and prayer, bear you heavenwards. Let your conversation be in heaven.

I know that I have as little power to elevate my soul to heaven, as a bar of iron has to mount in the air. But the love of Christ, as a powerful magnet, draws me thither. My cry shall therefore ever be, "Lord, draw me, and we will run after thee," Sol. Song 1:4. Amen.

www.ingramcontent.com/pod-product-compliance
Lightning Source LLC
Chambersburg PA
CBHW072012040426
42447CB00009B/1595